JUST WHO DO YOU THINK YOU ARE?

just who do you think you are?

THE POWER OF PERSONAL EVOLUTION

ALAN MESHER

SIRIUS CREATIONS INC.
PACIFIC PALISADES, CALIFORNIA

Sirius Creations Inc.

P.O. Box 1290

Pacific Palisades, CA 90272

Printed in the United States of America

10 9 8 7 6 5 4 3 2 1

Publishers Cataloging in Publication Data

Mesher, Alan.
   Just Who Do You Think You Are? The Power of Personal Evolution/ Alan Mesher.
      191 p.: 21 cm.
      ISBN 0-9660295-2-6
      1.Change (Psychology). 2. Self-help techniques. 3. Self-realization. I. Title.
      BF637
      158.1   200398357

ALSO BY ALAN MESHER

Journey of Love: A formula for Mastery and Miracles
The T Zone: The Path to Inner Power

Single copies may be ordered from:

Sirius Creations Inc.

P.O. Box 1290

Pacific Palisades, CA 90272

(310) 228·3110

or purchased directly on the internet at:

http://www.siriuscreations.com

orders@siriuscreations.com

COVER DESIGN: CATHI STEVENSON
TEXT DESIGN: LAURIE BURKE

ACKNOWLEDGEMENTS

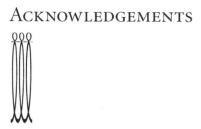

I would like to thank Jackie Peters for urging me to write this book.

I would like to thank Jackie Shaffers, Tanyia Kandohla-Mullens, Sean Kandohla-Mullens, Laura Hemmers, Mike Barry, and Lisa Monatlik for their reading of the material and their helpful observations, comments, and suggestions.

I would especially like to thank Nan Temkin Dudley for her astute copy editing of the manuscript and Robert Wilkinson for his sage comments in editing the early chapters.

I would further like to thank Laura Hemmers for dreaming up the title. Her idea was better than any of mine.

I would like to thank Cathi Stevenson of BookCover Express for her inspired cover design.

I would like to thank Laurie Burke of Subtext for her thoughtful text design and her great generosity in steering me to many helpful resources. Laurie always found the time in her busy schedule to address my concerns, many of which had nothing to do with text design.

I would like to thank Patricia Webb, manager of Starbucks in Pacific Palisades, CA., and her associate Yohana Solomon for providing a welcoming and friendly environment while I labored daily on this manuscript.

Finally, I would like to thank my son, Matthew, for the patience and maturity he displayed while I was absorbed in the creation of this work.

Having a great mother is a huge advantage in life.
I was more fortunate than most.
I had two.

I dedicate this book to my mother,
Francis Kramer Mesher,
and my dear friend,
Patricia Wilson.

Would that all people were as good, as compassionate and
loving, and as strong and true in their lives as these two
women were in theirs.

May God hold them in the gentle embrace of His infinite love
forever.

CONTENTS

PREFACE

Some four hundred years before the birth of Christ, the philosopher Socrates uttered his famous maxim. "The unexamined life," he said emphatically, "is not worth living." When Socrates was holding philosophical discussions in the marketplace of Athens, the world's population was only a tiny fraction of what it is today, and the technology of the times was limited to working in metal, wood, stone, and clay. People rose with the sun and went to bed when it set. Life had a defined rhythm and a deliberate pace.

Today we wrestle with such problems as overpopulation and a toxic environment, and while our advanced technology has improved the quality of our lives, it has also increased the speed of life and heightened the stress under which we all labor. Modern economic, technological, and social trends are relentlessly at work reformulating and redefining our civilization, forcing us to move at speeds far greater than those for which our nervous systems were designed. The increasing speed of life is neither a short-term phenomenon nor a one-time aberration from the norm, but has become a constant in our culture. Keeping up with the pace of change as well as the chronic demands that constant change places on our systems, has created a whole new set of problems for us to deal with.

One of these problems is that we rarely have time to reflect on life's purpose and meaning or to discover who we really are. What free time we do have is largely channeled into the endless assortment of mind numbing entertainments that our culture provides, but what relief we find in those diversions is of a temporary nature. Rather than creating a foundation of inner peace in what we do, we lurch instead from crisis to crisis. As our stress builds and our energy diminishes, our patience with one another disappears. We seldom listen and we rarely forgive. Instead, we accuse and blame, deepen our divisions, and contribute to the growing climate of conflict that is plaguing the world. When we go too fast in life two things happen: we lose our balance, and then we crash.

While the words of Socrates may be ancient, largely forgotten, and ignored, they have never been more relevant. If we are to build a better world, we must know who we really are. We have accomplished a great deal with our technology, but we have strayed far from ourselves in doing so. The price of our success has been the loss of our identity. The world is in crisis, and what we do to address that crisis may well determine the future course of civilization. If we are to have peace in the world, we must create peace within ourselves. If we are to find love, we must become love. If we are to find fulfillment, we must help others find theirs. If the world is to change, we must embody the change we seek.

I wrote *Just Who Do You Think You Are?* to help those who are ready discover their true identity. For more than two decades I have helped people balance their lives and move forward to greater success and inner fulfillment. The ideas and principles in this book come from that work. What my clients have taught me about their individual predicaments applies equally to us all.

The universal is mirrored in the particular. We are all human and have the same basic set of needs. These needs were programmed into us as a species when we were conceived and have stayed with us as we have grown and evolved as a race. The deepest of these needs is our eternal search to find out who we are. That quest is why we are here. We are all in pursuit of transformation, whether we realize it or not. Life is a quest for truth, light, and identity. The answer to that quest does not lay outside us, but rather, hidden deep within us. No one can do the work of transformation for us. This work we must do for ourselves. *Just Who Do You Think You Are?* is about walking the path of Light as directly, deeply, and powerfully as possible.

In writing this book I have referred to the Divine in masculine terms, as a He rather than a She. I have done this, not because I feel that the Divine power has a gender, but because it is simpler and more economical to speak in terms of one gender than to speak in terms of two. Likewise, in places where I could have said his and hers, I chose to use the masculine pronoun to refer to both genders because that is how it has been handled historically. I have followed that literary convention in order to economize my use of words and to make those sentences in which I could have said his or her less awkward.

If you find value in *Just Who Do You Think You Are?* please consider reading my previous book, *The T Zone: The Path to Inner Power.* *The T Zone* will deepen your understanding of unconscious dynamics and amplify your appreciation of what may truly happen when you heal your life.

Throughout this book I have cited the experiences of several clients to better illustrate important dynamics in the psyche. I have changed the names of these clients to protect their identity and privacy.

Resistance And Acceptance

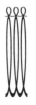

What we cannot accept makes us unhappy.
What makes us unhappy we resist.
What we resist, we struggle against.
What we struggle against binds us to it.
Whatever binds us, enslaves us.
Whatever enslaves us, shames us.
Whatever shames us, diminishes us.

Our failure to accept the way things are lies at the root
of our problems.
Our resistance makes us rigid with resentment.
It steals our clarity and power, and deprives us of
happiness.
What we cannot accept we draw to us and are doomed
to repeat, over and over again.

What we accept will change, because we have changed.
When there is no more resistance within us, our
behavior will not be polarizing.
Everything will flow toward balance and harmony.
Peace will prevail over conflict.

Forgiveness is the key to acceptance.
We can't forgive until we find the inner victim and
acknowledge our pain.

When we find our pain we must embrace it completely.
Until we become one with our pain we will be unable to
release it.

Knowing this, the wise man resolutely faces himself,
feels his pain fully, and goes free. He becomes strong
and complete.
Fearing this, the foolish man deceives himself, denies
his pain, and diminishes his power. He remains in
harm's way, beaten down by that which binds him.
Because of his self-deception he grows even weaker and
more incomplete. His rage never ends.

The world will become peaceful when we become
peaceful.
To find inner peace we must face ourselves, and remove
the source of our resistance.
It is far better to face our self than it is to continually
blame others for our predicament.
Blame makes the negative the ruling power in our lives.
When we find inner peace, the solutions to our
problems are clear and obvious.

The future of the world is in our hands.
If we don't find inner peace, who will?
We are the world.
When we save ourselves, we save the world.
The time to act is now, not later.
We are too close to losing the future.

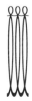

one THE SILENT EPIDEMIC

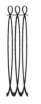

*I know of no more encouraging fact than the
unquestionable ability of a man to elevate his life by
conscious endeavor.*

Henry David Thoreau

Be the change you want to see in the world.

Mahatma Gandhi

Life is a risky business. We shine here for a short time then disappear. Permanence is an illusion. Everything in the physical world is temporary, subject to decline, decay, and dissolution, even the rocks and the stars and the sea.

We all know this, and yet we all ignore this. No one wants to dwell on the inevitable. It is too painful and disturbing. Instead, we build our lives, make our plans, and hope that good fortune will shine on us when we need it most. Despite the clarity of our intentions, the brilliance of our plans, and the sincerity of our prayers, our efforts to court success do not ultimately guarantee success. We cannot account for every possibility or prepare ourselves for what cannot be foreseen. While we all would like life to be orderly, predictable, happy, and secure what we least expect to happen is what often occurs. The only constant life ever brings us is constant change.

With the impermanent nature of reality operating relentlessly in the background, the only real security we can find in life is the light and consciousness we build within ourselves. If we cannot consistently count on something outside ourselves to save us, we must learn to rely on the inner light of our soul to guide us to safety and lead us to success.

Orthodox Religion, Mystic Tradition: Two Views of Human Nature

The great religions of the west have consistently taught their congregations that they are weak and sinful; that God exists outside of and separate from them; and that the church is their only legitimate avenue to redemption and salvation. Over time these teachings have created a deep sense of dependence on the church and a compelling, almost irreversible belief in personal guilt. To the extent that these teachings have empowered the church they have disempowered the individual. Instead of uplifting and transforming the masses these teachings have often cast doubt upon the nature of human potential.

We now live in a time when more people are better educated, affluent, and informed than ever before. The pace of social and technological change in the world continues to accelerate. Everything is in flux. The culture is rapidly changing. The old order is being questioned and challenged as it never was before. Nothing is sacred. The time of blind, unquestioning obedience is over. People are eager to improve their lives, find peace and happiness, and fulfill their potential. As more people seek to transform their lives they have come to the realization that guilt and dependence will not help them go forward but will lead instead to further weakness, confusion, and suffering. More and more people are determined to find their inner light and leave their pain and darkness far behind them.

The ancient wisdom traditions of both East and West have a different perspective on human nature and man's relationship to divine authority than the views offered by conventional religion. For thousands of years these wisdom teachings have said that the Divine light dwells in each of us and that there is no real separation between man and God but that which we create ourselves. The main purpose of life is to forge our connection to the Divine. As we develop that connection, the power of the Divine flows down into us. As that power flows into us it lifts us up, helping us evolve into the person we were always meant to be. As we continue to grow, and our capacity to hold more light expands, we become a conduit of unconditional love and compassion to those in need.

According to the mystic view of human nature we are not sinful, dependent, and weak, but extraordinary beings capable of great luminosity and unconditional love. If we are to fulfill our true potential the Divine does not want us to be wracked with guilt over our innate sinfulness, but rather, to find our oneness with Him. Where orthodox religions indoctrinated their followers into belief systems that may limit their inner potential, the ancient mystical traditions developed methods of personal transformation that fulfill that potential.

Access to our inner light is certainly a great advantage to have when we are faced with a rapidly changing world, great unrest, high stress, deepening anxiety, and a climate of contagious uncertainty. That advantage is one of the reasons why there has been so much interest in Eastern mysticism and alternate systems of transformation in the west.

Polarization

As a new century dawns, one worldwide trend is particularly worrisome and may have reached epidemic proportions already. This is the trend toward political, economic, religious, and social polarization that continues to grow unabated in every sphere of life. The gaps that divide us continue to grow larger, and the emotional distance that separates us continues to grow wider. There is little remaining cohesion to hold us together. What common ground we do share shrinks beneath our feet.

With every passing day and every new upheaval, these distances continue to grow, that cohesion continues to erode, and a peaceful future slips further from our grasp. Extreme selfishness has replaced respect for the common good. We have less in common than we ever have. Turmoil, hostility, and conflict are at high pitch, sweeping over our small planet with alarming ease. Nothing seems able to slow the rising wave of negativity. Everywhere, on every continent and in every country, people feel a deep sense of foreboding about the future. No one is immune from the corrosive anxiety, the loss of innocence, and the increasing toxicity of our times.

It is as if a dark tide were gathering its strength, while we stand helpless in the rising water, waiting for the deluge that seems certain to come. Many fear that this time it might be too late to save the world from itself. In the meantime, we stand shivering in the cold currents of our time, unprotected and vulnerable, facing a worldwide epidemic of conflict, polarization, frenzy, and rage.

The Negative Momentum of Our Times

When an individual acts out his rage there are no winners Everyone loses The impact of isolated incidents of violence contributes to the flood of darkness sweeping over the world and encourages others, who are also unstable and full of rage, to commit similar atrocities. Terrible acts committed by unstable people, lead to more unstable people committing terrible acts. This is one way a negative trend starts. The psychic atmosphere of the globe becomes polluted by the increasing sum of terrible acts and encourages ever more terrible atrocities.

The world is full of lost souls. If we lose sight of the inner person, we lose our way in life. "What does it profit a man," Christ once asked, "to gain the whole world and lose his soul?" The answer is devastatingly simple. It profits him nothing.

Where Are We Headed?

No one knows where we are headed, but we are running faster than we ever have to get there. Chaos? World War? A series of regional wars? The use of weapons of mass destruction? Chemical, biological, or nuclear attacks? Earth and climate changes? Pole shifts? Two hundred mile an hour winds swirling over the planet, destroying all plant life, most homes and buildings, and nearly all of us? Massive earthquakes? Volcanic eruptions? Tidal waves? Floods? Water appearing where it hasn't been seen in centuries? Planetary warming? Gaping holes in the ozone layer? Famine? Chronic drought? Starvation? Plagues? Incurable infectious diseases?

Presently, nearly two billion people in the world are without access to clean drinking water. Two hundred fifty thousand new babies are born everyday. Estimates suggest that by the year 2015 there will be 8.5 billion people on the planet, increasing the present population by nearly a third. Virtually all that growth will occur in the third world where there is not enough fresh water, food, housing, or economic opportunity as it is. The additional population will become a source of new crises and increased conflict that will impact the whole world. As it is, AIDS cases are rising dramatically in the third world and are beginning to climb again in America following a period of slow growth.

In the United States, over one third of the population now has Insulin Resistance Syndrome, a leading precursor of diabetes and heart disease. Sixty percent of the population is overweight. Statistics indicate that one out of two Americans will contract some form of cancer during their lifetime. If we do not destroy ourselves through ideological and cultural divides, limited economic opportunity, war, lack of food and clean water, we may well destroy ourselves by eating processed foods, packed with refined sugar and carcinogens, breathing toxic air, and drinking contaminated water.

Unfortunately, what we are doing to ourselves is only part of the saga in the growing epidemic of global imbalance. The other part of the story is what we have done to the earth's ecosystem. Because of our prolific capacity for heedless pollution, nature is fast losing her capacity to regenerate herself, and may one day fail to support us. The natural world is our foundation. Our continued existence is impossible without its embrace.

The Web of Life

Why is it that as human beings we hurt and destroy nearly everything we touch? Could it be because we are out of touch with our true nature and have no respect for or sensitivity to things, species, and people outside of ourselves? We're not the only show in town or the only species on the planet. When we uproot and destroy everything in our path in the name of profit and power, we sow the seeds of our own destruction. Life is a web, and all species on the planet, including us, are contained and connected within that web. Destroy one part of that intricate network and the web of life is suddenly out of balance.

Without systemic balance, all the individual elements of the web will eventually suffer. Interfere with the ability of several elements of the web to function as intended, and that suffering will come much faster and cut much deeper. We may well be at that point now. The overriding ecological question of our time is whether or not we have reached the point of no return. Is there still time for us to rise to the challenge, overcome the polarization that plagues us, and save ourselves and the ecosystem from overwhelming degradation?

Of course, the degradation of the ecosystem contributes to the rise of epidemics. When we rip the web of life asunder, pollute the environment, and make the world more toxic, we create the conditions for that toxicity to come back to haunt us. When we destroy our foundation, we put our future at risk. In a famous and controversial speech made in 1854, but not reported on until thirty-three years later, Chief Seattle of the Suquamish Indians was attributed with making the following remarks: "Whatever befalls the earth befalls the children of the earth. We did not weave the web of life; we are merely strands in it. Whatever we do to the web, we do to ourselves."

Karma and Accountability

We do not operate in a vacuum. What we do to others and what we do to the world, life one day will do to us. We are all accountable for our actions. Everything we do, the good as well as the bad, will eventually come home to us. Our actions are an investment in our future. We never escape our karma. Rumi, the great mystical poet of the fourteenth century, put the notion of karmic accountability in these terms: "If you cause injury to someone, you draw that same injury to yourself."

Taking this fundamental truth under consideration, our strategy should be to proceed thoughtfully and deliberately in our lives. We should be compassionate, sensitive, and clear in what we do and why we do it. Being deliberate and in control of our emotions is far superior to being impulsive and controlled by momentary desires. The wise person lives by The Golden Rule and will "do unto others as he would have them do unto him."

If our actions have been destructive to other people's well-being, all our attempts to deny our activities, discredit others, and distance ourselves from the repercussions of our actions will prove futile in the end. There is no escaping the long reach of universal law. The Law of

Consequences, or Karma, makes no exceptions for anyone. We are all equal under that law. Karma has no favorites. God cannot be bribed or placated. What we do now determines what life will bring us later. We are responsible for our destiny.

Karma and the Long Term

Sometimes, however, it might seem that universal law does not work as advertised. Many ruthless killers throughout history became powerful and rich, and led privileged lives. Some ruled countries. A few created empires. Several were celebrated. Where, then, are the consequences to their actions? They seem to have been rewarded for their inhumanity rather than punished for their crimes.

What must not be forgotten is that universal law applies to the long term as well as the short term. The consequences for actions against humanity are not always immediate. The Law of Consequences determines the timing of karmic events. It manifests our karma when it deems that the conditions are right for us to be confronted with the experience we created for ourselves.

Richard Nixon, for example, won many elections by spreading lies and ruthlessly destroying the reputations of his opponents. In his early political career it seemed like a successful strategy, enabling him to swiftly climb the political ladder from congressman to Vice-President of the United States. His karma did not come back to haunt him until the zenith of his political career when he was re-elected President of the United States in a landslide victory in 1970, winning every state's electoral votes but Massachusetts. Then came Watergate. Two years after his triumphant re-election, he was forced to resign his high office in disgrace. The man who had destroyed the reputation and careers of others had now destroyed his own.

If Nixon's karma had come back to him when he had first created it, his humiliation would have occurred on a local scale, been noted in the local papers, and then quickly forgotten. Instead, the Law of Consequences waited until he had reached the pinnacle of his career and attained the high office he had lusted after for decades before manifesting his karma. His humiliation occurred on the world stage under the glare of the world media, rather than on the inside pages of the local paper. The Law of Consequences is very patient. Its timing is impeccable, and it never fails to find us.

Refining the Soul

From the Divine perspective, we are embodied souls having all kinds of experiences in the physical world in order to facilitate our growth. The business of evolution is the refining of the soul, and part of that refining process involves learning right from wrong and developing a conscience to guide us. In this way the karma we create as we go forward will be positive and accelerate our evolution rather than impede it. If we don't develop a strong ethical nature, we run the danger, much like Richard Nixon did, of being chronically stuck in destructive patterns that will continue to create negative consequences in our lives. Without a moral compass to steer us we will generate more imbalances in our lives and add to the overwhelming problem of imbalance in the world.

The Law of Consequences is not a law of retaliation, although it might seem that way. Rather, it is actually a way of teaching responsibility and accountability. Life gives us free will. Within certain parameters we can do what we want, but we are also accountable for our actions. What better way to learn the difference between right and wrong than to be forced to suffer the same fate we may have forced on someone else?

Mirror Images

Karmic experiences then, are often the mirror images of what we once did to someone else. They reflect our lessons back to us. Though it may be difficult to find the hidden cause of our dilemmas, painful experiences that come into our lives unexpectedly are often the result of past sins of commission or omission. The reverse of course, is also true. Helping someone in need will bring help to us in the future when we need it most.

Wherever we go and whatever we do, the Law of Consequences always accompanies us, registering all that we do. The Law doesn't create our karma. We do that. The Law makes us responsible for what we do, whether or not we want that responsibility. We create our future by what we do now, by how we treat other people as we move through life.

The Law of Consequences and the Soul

Since the Law of Consequences deals more with the soul than the personality, it is not limited to working out someone's karma during the lifetime in which that karma occurred. The law is patient and may wait for another incarnation before it inserts that soul into the karmic situation it had created previously for itself.

I once had a client come to me, a psychotherapist, who had recently embarked on a new relationship with a wonderful woman. He came to resolve issues of long standing that had little to do with his new relationship. Despite the issues that he wanted to address, when he got on my healing table the spiritual light that I channeled into his body brought to the surface an unknown strand of karma that had been hidden in his soul for hundreds of years. This karmic strand was from a lifetime in the fourteenth century of which he had no previous awareness. In that life he had been a soldier in charge of protecting a village from the attacks of roving marauders. One day he and his men were out on patrol when the thieves sneaked around them and attacked the village. They killed all the men and carried off the women and children to sell into slavery. When my client and his men returned to the village they encountered a ghastly scene of death and destruction. My client was devastated. Not only had he failed to protect the village, but the raiders had also carried off the woman he loved and was betrothed to marry.

He regrouped his men and at dawn the next day they followed the thieves to their stronghold in the mountains. They arrived late in the afternoon and hid in a nearby forest waiting for the cover of night to attack. Unfortunately, the bandits had anticipated the soldier's plan and sent several scouting parties into the woods to search for them. The soldiers were located almost as soon as they arrived. Whatever element of surprise they might have had was now lost. Their attack was a complete disaster. My client was killed during the battle. He had tried to rescue his

9

beloved and failed, sacrificing his life in a vain attempt to save her and the other women and children from the village.

When my client returned to normal consciousness he was overcome by emotion. The past life he had just experienced explained the deep love he had felt immediately on meeting the woman he was now involved with and the terrible feelings he experienced whenever they parted. Each time she left him he was sure that he would never see her again. She too had fallen in love with him immediately and shared the same terrible feeling of loss whenever they parted. Now he knew why his feelings were so powerful and why his fear of losing her was so strong. She was the woman he had loved and lost long ago. The Law of Consequences had brought them together again to live out the love they had not been able to experience and complete more than six hundred years earlier. A lost opportunity had come full circle, becoming a new chance to complete the past and heal an ancient wound.

Greed and Universal Law

There is, of course, another side to the karmic coin. My client and his partner had been brought together to experience a beauty that had never had the chance to bloom in the time of its conception. Since the energy between them had been pure and loving, their encounter with each other in this lifetime rekindled that love. Most people, however, are motivated by factors that are not as pure. For example, those whose greed is stronger than their conscience often refuse to consider the way Universal Law functions or to admit that it even exists. For the greedy person, it's always about today, never tomorrow. The greedy person rarely considers the consequences of his actions and will often deny that any correlation exists between what he does now and what he draws to himself later. The greedy person is too engrossed in the overwhelming demand of his own need to see how his actions impact other people or to care that he has hurt them. Profit and self-advancement are more important to him than doing what is right and honorable. He considers the notion of the web of life irrelevant and immaterial. It is his focus on self, profit, and the present, to the neglect of other people's well-being, and the future cost of that neglect upon the environment, that leads him to continually inflict suffering upon the world.

Greed, of course, is a form of self-involvement and heightened self-ishness. All self-involvement is a sign of emotional immaturity and an expression of need. Greed then, is need's instrument. The overwhelming sense of need that drives greed makes it blind to everything but what it desires in that particular moment. It is rarely interested in anyone else's well-being because it is too preoccupied with its own distorted needs to see beyond its self-gratification. Greed is never very clear or far seeing. It has little sense of proportion and less conscience. It doesn't care who it hurts or how it hurts them, as long as it gets what it wants.

The survival of the planet, however, is a long-term concern that involves all of us. The sustainability of the environment requires a group effort. Greed is the enemy of that effort. Greed's focus on self-concern to the detriment of everyone else promotes polarization, conflict, and hostility. Greed is one of the major causes of imbalance in the world and one of the great enemies of the future.

Greed and Desire

"All people on the planet are children," wrote the poet Rumi, "except for a very few. No one is grown up except those free of desire." Desire is the ally of greed. They are like the right and left hand of the same person. When they combine in our nature they fan the flame of selfishness and extinguish common sense. If we lose our common sense we will often ignore our innate sense of right and wrong. Without a moral compass to guide us it is all too easy to abandon ourselves to the most destructive elements in our nature.

I once knew a man who had been a fine athlete in his youth. As an adult he became a high school teacher and a football coach. One fateful night he found someone else's credit card. The temptation to use that card burned in his mind for days and in the end proved too much for him to overcome. He went on a buying spree, purchasing several luxury items he could not afford on his teacher's salary. Needless to say, he was eventually caught, arrested, and punished. His actions destroyed his reputation and

11

led to great personal humiliation. Desire and greed led an otherwise decent man down a frighteningly fast path to self-destruction.

Where the Marriage of Desire and Greed Begins

The collaboration of desire and greed begins when we decide we want something we don't have. By focusing intensely on what we want, we soon find that we can't bear to live without it. What we don't have consumes us, and our desire for what we don't have incites our greed to go and get it. What we want becomes what we must have. When something enters our "must have" zone, we will do almost anything to get it. The mixture of greed and desire exacerbates our neediness and adds an element of unhappiness and desperation to an already volatile combination of negative motivations. The conjunction of desire, greed, need, and unhappiness can easily overwhelm our common sense and cause our undoing. Greed and desire flourish when we do not know who we really are and are not centered in our true identity. It is only when we are centered in our true identity that we are relieved of greed's temptations.

When greed and desire dominate our conscious minds, short-term, selfish thinking dominates our lives. When we lose sight of the big picture, focusing solely on our own gratification, we are primed to cause repetitive injury to the web of life and create karmic repercussions in our own lives. When greed and desire are in the ascendant in our lives we will be unhappy and out of balance. When they are the dominant forces in the world, the world will be full of suffering. If the level of imbalance in the world continues to grow, how can we possibly protect the future and build a better world?

The Most Insidious Epidemic of Our Time

The most insidious epidemic of our time is the lack of inner balance that exists in nearly all of us and is reflected in the world around us. When the population of the planet was much less than it is today, when the available technology was much cruder, the damage done to the web of life was repairable by nature. That is no longer the case. There are now too many of us with too much internal toxicity and too much technology to continue on in the same way as before. Personal toxicity and advanced technology present a frightening combination of unpredictable factors that threaten the future of this planet. There is too little margin of error in our endeavors to tolerate much more thoughtless greed.

While we cannot legislate consciousness, we can choose to rectify our own lack of balance and find our true center. When we are centered we are better positioned to deal with the challenges of life and the particular stresses of our time. If enough of us become centered and clear, together we will create a clear and radiant energy field that will help the world overcome the negative trends now dominating it. There can be no balance in the world until there is more balance in each of us. In order to find the balance we need we must overcome our attachments to greed and desire.

The Two Major Aspects of the Human Bio-System

There is only one certain way to restore our internal balance. We must transform our nature by clearing the unconscious emotional toxicity that pollutes it. Most of us live in the gulf of confusion that separates the human from the Divine. If we are to fulfill our potential, we must find a way to incorporate the Divine elements of our nature into our conscious experience. In most of us, the Divine elements exist more as a promise and a hope than as a tangible reality. The challenge we face is how to stretch our consciousness toward the Divine. We won't escape the gulf of confusion we inhabit until we do. Fortunately, we have been designed by our Creator to accomplish this very task. When God gave us a body, He also gave us a soul and spirit. We have a dual nature and are a unique combination of physical substance and Divine energy. Our job is to unite the two and make them one.

The physical elements of our system are designed to last a lifetime, but no more. They are mortal. On the other hand, the supra-physical aspects of our system are designed to last for eternity. They are immortal. Therefore, while the physical part of us is destructible and will die, the larger part of us that we do not see and rarely experience is indestructible and will never perish.

The physical components of our system include the brain, the skeletal structure and the physical body with its various organ systems, such as the circulatory, respiratory, endocrine, immune, digestive, muscular, and nervous systems.

The supra-physical elements of our system include the electromagnetic field, or aura, that encircles the physical body, the seven major chakras (an Indian term that means a spinning wheel of light) that exist just outside the front of the body, and the subtle nervous system, composed of the meridians and the nadis, that is located within the physical body. (For a complete and detailed visual representation of the supra-physical elements of the human system please view the work of the artist Alex Grey as they appear in his book of remarkable paintings, *Sacred Mirrors*.)

The electromagnetic field contains the energies of mind (as differentiated from the brain), emotion, soul, and spirit. These aspects of consciousness are represented in the electromagnetic field as bands of light and color that encircle the physical body. The band of the emotional nature is the band closest to the body. Next to it is the sheath of the mind, followed by the sheath of the soul. The band of the spirit is the band farthest from the body. The bands of the mental nature and soul lie between those of the emotional nature and the spirit.

The ancient Yogis of India had an interesting aphorism they used to describe the relationship between the mind and the body. "The mind is not contained in the body," they said, "but the body is contained in the mind." At first glance this aphorism may not seem to make much sense, but when we think of the mind and body in terms of the aura, it makes perfect sense. Since the energies of the mind are located in the electromagnetic field surrounding the body, the body is literally contained within the mind, much like an egg is contained within its shell. The physical brain is the central receiving station for the mind as well as the processor for the ideas that emanate from the mental sheath of the aura.

Unlike the energies of the mind, soul and spirit, the seven chakras are not bands of light and color surrounding the body in successive layers but are, rather, spinning wheels of light located in specific locations just in front of the physical body. The chakras transform and distribute the energy from the electromagnetic field into the physical body in order to sustain the body and regulate its many systems.

The subtle nervous system is made up of the acupuncture meridians, charted by ancient Chinese seers, and the nadis, charted by ancient Indian sages. The meridians and nadis are both microscopic channels through which the subtle energy that has been stepped down through the chakras is distributed throughout the body. The main focus of the meridians is the health of the physical body, while the nadis are concerned with the individual's spiritual evolution. Just as plants need sun to grow, we need spiritual light to evolve.

The flow of subtle energy moves down through the various levels of our consciousness, starting at the spiritual level then down through the soul, mind, chakras, and, finally, into the meridians and nadis. At each succeeding level, the energy is stepped down so that the physical body might be able to handle the influx of power without having its circuits blown.

The Conscious Gateway

Self-actualization occurs when spiritual light is consciously introduced into the energy channels of the subtle nervous system through meditation and is then directed to rise in a disciplined manner through the chakras, starting with the base chakra at the bottom of the spine system and culminating in the chakra above the top of the head. When all of the seven chakras are opened, synchronized, and vibrating at their highest optimal level, they form a conscious gateway to the realms of the soul and spirit that is sealed off from our awareness until the gateway is created. That gateway is of supreme importance in our evolution. Fully opened, it is the vehicle for developing a strong soul connection and moving beyond the gulf of confusion that plagues most people. The spiritual light that flows up the gateway to our spirit, there to be answered by an even greater stream of spiritual energy flowing down from the spirit to our conscious mind, completes that higher connection. The great mystery of who we really are cannot be revealed until we make that connection.

It is important to stress that making that higher connection is a two-fold process. We must direct energy through the gateway to our spirit. Our spirit must then answer by sending Divine energy back down to us. Our spirit may not answer right away. The reason for this potential delay is that the spirit will not respond until it is sure that we are ready to be embraced by a higher degree of unconditional love than we have heretofore experienced and accept our unity with life. In its wisdom the spirit monitors our state of readiness and protects us from receiving too much power too soon. It responds to our call for unity when we are ready to know who we really are.

When that higher connection does occur and our conscious mind is united with our soul and spirit, we become whole in ways we have never been whole before. The integration of the physical and supra-physical elements of our system is the platform for the next stage in our evolution: the birth of spiritual power, the beginning of Self-realization, and the advent of a growing luminosity. In this stage, we will come to know our Divine connection, our relationship to all things, and our true identity.

Unfortunately, most people never become conscious of their supra-physical elements and thus, never consciously evolve. They never realize who they really are, for they have only developed a relatively small part of their nature. In most people, that means they will go no farther than where their intellect can take them. Many people of high intelligence fail to realize that the soul and spirit begin where the intellect ends, that their true identity lies beyond the borders of rational thought.

The soul and spirit are the transcendent parts of our nature. Our true identity is housed there, as is our life purpose. Until we integrate the physical and supra-physical aspects of our system, our truth is dormant and our luminosity undiscovered.

Higher Consciousness and the Collective Consciousness

A strong link exists between our personal consciousness and the collective consciousness of the society in which we live. Each sphere of consciousness continuously impacts the other. Neither sphere is static or separate. The collective consciousness of the world's democracies, for example, is more fluid than we might imagine. It always responds to an infusion of consciousness from awakened individuals. When enough of us raise our consciousness and integrate the two major aspects of our system, the collective consciousness will gradually open up to incorporate the changes we have made within ourselves.

Throughout history there have been individuals whose teachings and truths were spiritually powerful enough to change the collective consciousness. The teachings of Krishna, Moses, Buddha, Christ, and Mohammed changed the world and continue to impact the lives of billions of people today, yet their teachings alone are not enough to help today's world emerge from its current impasse. Until we become the change we seek, the world cannot move into the light.

The Gulf Between Belief and Truth

For a truth to be powerful and relevant, it must be lived. If we do not live the truth, we cannot experience it but only believe it. Our inability to live the truth creates a gulf between what we may profess to believe and who we are. One of the tragic realities of life is that many of us have spent too much time in the gulf of confusion that occupies the space between belief and true identity. The good news is that we can move beyond belief, choose to live our truth, and become more than we have been. We cross the gulf of confusion to safety when we transform our shadow and begin to live our truth, rather than continuing to trudge down the worn road of our toxicity.

Why We Are Not Helpless

We can change the world together. As individuals we are not helpless. At our deepest levels of consciousness, we share a beauty of spirit and a unity with all of life that is powerful and redemptive. What we do to discover our deeper selves counts for more than we might imagine. If we can arrive together at that deep space, nothing will be able to stop the good from rising again in the world.

When enough of us succeed in transforming ourselves, the collective consciousness will hold more light and goodness. Together, we can be the levers of change that draw down the power from above. When we open ourselves to a higher power and a Divine source, we are no longer alone without voice or influence. We become, instead, a positive center of light, and when our personal light is turned on, the vast impersonal power of the Divine can flow through us and reach out to help others.

If we do not find our identity and actualize our purpose, we will not find a lasting fulfillment in life, and the thing we were truly meant to do in the world will not get done. One of the great tragedies of life is that too few of us accomplish what we were meant to do. If more of us were to find our way to our true identity and purpose, we would all be much closer to God. The Divine light would be everywhere, and evil would be blocked permanently from entering the world.

Aspiration

Our aspiration to grow is the key to bringing down the higher power that will accelerate our evolution and help us discover who we really are. Aspiration is a magnetic power and a potent force that used correctly will increase our inner light and power. When our aspiration for the truth is sincere, it attracts to us what we need to grow. We can't grow unless we are nurtured by spiritual energy. When a sincere and loving call goes up, the power to heal one's inner wounds and restore peace in the world comes flowing back down. In the spiritual world, like attracts like. Christ instructed his followers how to use universal law. "Knock and it shall be opened," he exhorted. "Ask and ye shall receive." When we turn to God with a pure heart and a clear mind, God turns to us. That is the power of aspiration.

Unfortunately, the reverse is also true. Until we embrace our paradoxes and do the therapeutic inner work necessary to resolve our personal inconsistencies, our consciousness will retain its dark and toxic secrets, and the collective consciousness will remain permeated with lethal influences. The gulf of sorrow and confusion that consumes so much of the energy and consciousness in the world will remain intact. If we do not aspire upwards, God cannot intervene in our affairs. If we do not choose to grow, God will leave us to our fate. We are the levers of change. We either reach for our destiny and rise in the light, or we contract in the darkness of our anguish and fall to the fate we have created collectively.

We are the only ones who can bring down the forces from above to change the world. The ability to be a conduit of Divine power is a particularly human gift and a profound responsibility. If we don't take on this high work, who will? This is our planet; its well-being is in our hands. These are our lives; our futures and those of our children are at stake. The time to change the way things are is now, not later.

Critical Mass

The notion that a critical mass of consciousness can change the collective consciousness is not a new one. This idea emerged in the nineteen seventies when researchers in the wilds of Japan noticed that a few monkeys in the group they were observing began to wash their potatoes before eating them. Soon other monkeys in the group joined in this new behavior until approximately one hundred monkeys were washing their potatoes before they ate them. When the number of monkeys washing their potatoes in Japan reached one hundred, researchers in other remote regions of the world reported that the groups of monkeys they were observing also had begun to wash their potatoes before eating them.

Almost overnight, the behavior of an entire species, stretched over several continents, changed. This phenomenon of a sudden evolutionary shift in species behavior became known as The Hundredth Monkey theory.

The Hundredth Monkey theory contained two noteworthy ideas. One was the concept of critical mass. The other was the idea of morphogenesis. A British theoretical biologist, Rupert Sheldrake, theorized that the one hundred monkeys in the study represented the critical mass necessary to transform the invisible field that regulated the behavior of the entire species. Once the invisible regulating field shifted, monkeys all over the world reacted to that change by altering their eating habits. Sheldrake called his theory of an invisible regulating field morphogenesis.

The Hundredth Monkey theory with its ideas of critical mass and morphogenesis may provide an important clue to our future. If we are to make ourselves whole and fulfill our destiny, we must find our inner person and from that center of dynamic and magnetic force call down the inner light that will transform our lives. If enough of us engage in this endeavor, together we will create the critical mass needed to change the world. We will know we have reached critical mass when a shared center emerges, a common consensus is reached, and things in the world begin to change for the better. The morphogenic field that may in theory regulate human behavior might then encourage a new trend among the masses to seek personal growth and evolution.

¶ The Juxtaposition of Opposites

In times of conflict, darkness, and moral decay, seeking the light is a natural reflex. Salvation has a higher priority when life is less certain and the future less secure. God becomes more important when the negative forces at play in the world threaten to overrun us. As the darkness threatening us becomes greater, the urge to find comfort in God grows stronger.

We are not helpless. Everyone has a role to play in the great drama of life. We are here to grow and elevate our consciousness. We help the world get better when we get better. Each of us carries a piece of the world on our shoulders, and the fate of the world is our collective responsibility. We cannot fulfill our unique role in that responsibility until we find our real self and activate our higher purpose.

The Septimius Syndrome

In ancient times there was a Roman Emperor named Septimius Severus. Septimius was highly educated for his times, extremely intelligent, charismatic, handsome, and polished. He spoke several languages, studied literature and philosophy in Athens, and later became a lawyer in Rome. Long before he became the Emperor, he was thought of as one of the most brilliant minds in Rome. As a soldier and general, he was known for his daring and ruthlessness.

In 193 AD Rome was in political turmoil. The Emperor Com–
modus, son of Marcus Aurelius, had recently been assassinated. After
his assassination and the assassination of his successor, Pertinax, the
Praetorian Guard decided to auction off the office of the Emperor to
the highest bidder. The unfortunate winner of the Emperor sweepstakes
was a senator named Didius Julianus, who had been talked into bidding
for the office of Emperor by his wife and daughter. Julianus agreed to
pay each member of the Praetorian guard five thousand drachmas to become Emperor. Shortly after Julianus's installation, however, Septimius
decided that he wanted to be the Emperor. He also knew that other
Roman generals were thinking the same thing. So he seized the moment, marched his legions on Rome, and took control of the empire
with hardly a struggle.

During his takeover, a tribune in Septimius's service found Julianus
cowering in a palace bathroom and beheaded him. After his ascension
to imperial power, Septimius executed many more senators. He ruled
the Roman Empire with a strong hand for eighteen years, becoming the
most famous, powerful, and wealthiest man of his age.

On his deathbed in York, England in 211 AD after an extensive
military campaign in Caledonia (Scotland), Septimius had a chilling
revelation. In a moment of clarity, he saw the real worth of his life and
remarked, "I have been everything, and it is worth nothing." *

⁓ While Septimius may have been everything, he had failed to find
himself until it was too late to nurture his soul. He had fulfilled his desires
and taken from life all that his vast appetites had demanded, but it hadn't
been enough. His accomplishments and acquisitions had never relieved
the burden of his inner darkness. All his power, wealth, and fame had done
was obscure his emptiness and dissatisfaction with life. At the end, when
his moment of truth came the great wealth he had accumulated and the
power and fame he had seized mocked him. No time remained to burn
out the darkness in his soul that tormented him: no time to turn on his
inner light, redeem himself, or clear his karma. He went to his death internally bankrupt, the inner person starving, incomplete, and unfulfilled.
His life of external magnificence had been a life of internal failure.

* Durant, Will, *Caesar and Christ*, 622

Septimius had controlled an empire and decided the fates of entire populations, but he had never found real freedom. He had conquered the world but never conquered himself. He had been too in love with power to bother with his soul. In the end, his love of power had not liberated him, but had, rather, enslaved him. Unfortunately for Septimius, his failure to find himself was not the end of his journey but only it's beginning. In addition to neglecting his inner person, he had generated a great deal of negative karma that would have to be worked out in future lives.

Choices

Life is about the choices we make. Those choices determine our future. The wise person chooses to advance his evolution and contribute to the common good. The foolish person wastes his time wallowing in the gulf of confusion, creating more negative karma that will slow his progress toward life's inevitable goal. It is far better to discover the light within us and walk the path of wisdom while we still have the time to travel far down that path. It does no good to come too late to this work.

two THE CRUCIAL LINK

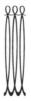

*Your vision will become clear only when you look into
your heart...Who looks outside dreams. Who looks
inside awakens.*

Carl Gustaf Jung

*Every individual has a place to till in the world and is
important in some respect, whether he chooses to be so
or not.*

Nathaniel Hawthorne

*First they ignore you, then they laugh at you, then they
fight you, then you win.*

Mahatma Gandhi

The world breaks from its moorings. The pace of life and the stress of
living grow in quantum leaps. Even though the sense of stability in the
world seems to be diminishing, relatively few people have begun to consciously develop the vital link to their soul. The future consequence of
the failure to act in one's highest interest is that many will be without
access to their inner center when they need it most.

Establishing a strong, clear link to our soul marks a crucial stage in
our evolution. It is this step that definitively separates those of us who
are whole from those who are wounded. If we choose to take this step,
we can move forward to heal ourselves and elevate our lives.

Soul Contact

When we consciously develop our connection to our soul we become peaceful, clear, and strong. These three qualities of soul contact provide a stabilizing bulwark against life's constant challenges. When we have these qualities the pressures of life will not break us. We will be able to stand up to hostile challenges and beat them back without losing our inner center or relinquishing our power. Every challenge we face will serve to make us stronger and wiser. Each success we have will increase our light and deepen our faith in ourselves,

The reason why soul contact makes us peaceful and clear is that the soul is at one with a higher power. It is eternal and fears nothing. It knows joy, and is filled with dynamic power and creative energy. Death cannot touch it, scare it, or destroy it. The soul is our link to the continuity of life. Our other assets come and go. Sometimes we profit from our material endeavors. Sometimes we fail, but regardless of what we may have accumulated or lost, when we die we will surrender all of our material assets. However, we never surrender our soul. It counts in life, and it counts after our physical life is over.

The Rising Tide of Fear

When our soul connection is dormant a recurrent sense of self-doubt and repeated questions of self-worth often rumble through our system. Those doubts and questions are like a major breach in a line of military fortifications. They leave us unprotected and allow many forms of fear to seep into our psyche. Fear is highly contagious when we do not have a strong inner center to defeat it. Fear feeds the negative, champions the hysterical, breeds confusion and paranoia, and exacerbates the tide of chaos running rampant in the world. Meanwhile, peace is almost nowhere to be found, neither in countries nor in individuals. The world becomes more polarized daily, and the voices raised above the growing din grow shriller. If the power of the negative continues to grow, where will we find our hope for the future? If the power of the negative mutates into new crises and the speed of its proliferation increases, what kind of world will we be passing on to our children? Will the future take care of itself if we go on blindly as we are doing and ignore the perils of the present?

We are all that stands between the rising tide of negativity in this world and progressive waves of conflict, chaos, and destruction. If we are wise and act together, we can generate the necessary critical mass to create a new positive trend, and we will be in time to make a difference. If we choose to forge the vital link to our souls, we will be strong enough and light enough to ease the massive pressure in the world.

If, on the other hand, we choose not to heal our lives, we are actually increasing the negative pressure in the world, making it that much tougher for the planet to heal and move forward to peace and safety. When the world is as polarized as it is today, there is no place to hide. Either we add to its polarization by neglecting our obligation to face our own darkness, or we contribute to its salvation by choosing to develop our inner light.

Soul contact has the capacity to transform negativity, reduce its threat, and slow its progress until it dies out altogether. The solution to what ails the world is as political as it is spiritual. If we find our wholeness, we can stand together in the light, united in our will to serve a high and loving purpose, and build the momentum to move forward, creating a peaceful and productive world.

When to Turn the Other Cheek and When Not To

Sometimes, when we are confronted with negativity in a personal context, the best course of action is non-action. Rather than getting drawn into a situation where the goal of our opponent is to taunt us into doing something foolish that will be used against us later, the wisest choice we can make is to not react in any way. If we don't permit ourselves to be drawn into a toxic embrace we can't be showered with toxic energy. Since no blow has been struck, we're under no obligation to defend ourselves. If we can maintain our self-control and not let our ego react as our adversary hopes it will, we will escape the danger he hopes to bring our way. In this kind of situation it is best to do as Christ advised and turn the other cheek. Keep cool. Do not react. Move on.

There are also times when we cannot afford to turn the other cheek and walk away but instead must take a stand and actively resist evil.

Sometimes, the right way is to stand and fight against an encroaching darkness in order to create a lasting peace and a freedom that endures. ╭ During World War Two, for example, many in India wanted Nazi Germany to win the war. Those who supported this position did so because they felt that if the Nazis won the war, the British would be forced out of India. While this may have been true, what they failed to realize was that if the Nazis replaced the British in India things would get worse for the Indian people, not better. Others wanted to apply Gandhi's philosophy on non-violence to opposing a potential Nazi invasion, even though Gandhi himself had said that ahimsa, or non-violence, would not work against the Nazis because they were an immoral political force with no conscience.

Like Gandhi, Sri Aurobindo, an Indian spiritual teacher of wide vision, also saw the folly in either supporting a Nazi invasion or opposing it with non-violence. Aurobindo, moreover, perceived the Second World War as part of an ongoing cosmic struggle of good versus evil in the world. Nazi Germany had to be opposed and defeated or the world would be shrouded in darkness and the flame of freedom extinguished everywhere. With the outbreak of hostilities he was certain that the fate of the world hung in the balance. In keeping with his vision, Aurobindo raised money for the British war effort and called on his fellow Indians to actively fight the Nazis, not with non-violence but with armed force.

Aurobindo's strong and vocal support for the British was most remarkable considering that as a young man he had been a firebrand and a political radical, extolling the use violence to secure India's independence from British rule. However, instead of securing India's freedom he had been captured by the British and tried for sedition. If he had been convicted of the charges brought against him he would have been executed, but he was acquitted instead. His acquittal marked his renunciation of violence and the beginning of his spiritual path.

Although Aurobindo had been devoted to peace for two decades before the war began, he knew that non-violence as a defensive strategy would insure a potential Nazi conquest of India rather than defeat it.

Faced with a ruthless foe, he resolved to stand and fight the tide of evil that was determined to overwhelm the world. Peace at any price was simply too high a price to pay for a peace that would be intolerable.

The Munich Pact

This truth was never more evident than in the early days of the war. In September 1938, Neville Chamberlain, the Prime Minister of Great Britain, attempted to appease Hitler and forestall further conflict by conceding the Sudetenland to him. The Sudetenland was a region of disputed territory in Czechoslovakia that contained a large German speaking population. Hitler was delighted to accept Chamberlain's concession, which the parties formalized in a treaty of non-aggression, known as the Munich Pact. Chamberlain then made a famous speech proclaiming "peace in our time." Unfortunately, that peace lasted only a short time. In March of 1939 Hitler invaded Czechoslovakia and then rolled over the rest of Europe. In Britain, Chamberlain's policy of appeasement brought down his government and returned Winston Churchill to power.

For many years before the war began, Churchill, like Aurobindo, had seen the threat of Nazi Germany for what it was. Both men took unpopular positions far in advance of their fellow countrymen. They both knew it was folly to appease an evil that sought the destruction of freedom and liberty.

Life is Struggle

Life, really, is always a struggle of one sort or another. We must fight against the stupidity, intolerance, prejudice, and hatred that are so entrenched in the world. We must also fight the negative qualities that are firmly entrenched within our own nature and constantly seeking to undermine us. Our greatest ally in the battles of life is the hidden power of our soul. When we overcome our negative ego and its urge to exert control over all that it can, we are unstoppable. When we have built the link to our soul, we stand in the true light of our being.

Moses, Christ, Krishna, Buddha, Mohammed, Gandhi, and Mother Teresa all had the very real advantage of that link. They knew who they were; they knew what their true purpose was, and they had the support of a higher power in fulfilling that purpose. In their work and in their lives they demonstrated what can be accomplished when we find our real self and discover our true purpose.

No one individual can lead the world out of its present morass. The world is too large, the problems we face too complex. But together we can stand up, and joined by a clear and loving purpose, we can heal ourselves and help the world move forward to a better future for all.

Gandhi and Self-discipline

The story of Mahatma Gandhi and his campaign to free India from the yoke of British colonialism is a case in point. When Gandhi returned to India from his sojourn in South Africa, he traveled by train around the Indian subcontinent and witnessed firsthand the great suffering caused by the widespread poverty of the Indian people. His initial plan was to help India overcome her impoverishment. As he moved forward to implement constructive economic change he soon realized that British rule was a main impediment to the economic aspirations of the Indian people. In time, his campaign for economic freedom became a movement for political freedom from British rule. Freeing India from the yoke of British rule became his life purpose. In order to reach that goal, Gandhi realized that he had to conquer his shadow and find his center so that the light of his soul might shine through. Self-discipline was among the important qualities that Gandhi cultivated in himself to reach that end.

In the long years of the struggle for Indian independence, Gandhi never wavered in his determination to reach his goal. He maintained his poise, rarely lost his self-control, and disciplined himself not to react to challenging events in a negative manner. Instead he would respond as positively and forthrightly as he could. He never sacrificed his commitment to the truth or compromised his principles. The final result of Gandhi's quest was inspiring and miraculous. He defeated a great empire peacefully, without violence. His only weapons were the truth in his soul and the strength of his character.

Through the years of struggle Gandhi had deliberately forged a very deep soul connection. He possessed inner peace, strength, and great clarity, qualities that helped him to understand who he was and what he was about. He clearly had a mission that required great strength and courage on the one hand, and little ego on the other. These attributes were amplified by the unconditional love that flowed through him. His love for all people, combined with his deep spirituality, created an opening in his energy system that magnetically pulled Divine love down from above, and distributed that energy to everyone within his sphere of influence. Wherever Gandhi went, whether to a prison or a podium, Divine love went with him. He had direct access to a higher authority and Divine support for his mission. With that support, Gandhi fulfilled his mission.

Stalin and Hitler

While Gandhi was busy using non-violence and satyagraha, or soul force, to emancipate the Indian people from under the yoke of British rule, Stalin and Hitler were busy using terror to consolidate their totalitarian grasp on power. Where Gandhi freed his people with little loss of life, Stalin and Hitler killed with impunity. Stalin was responsible for the deaths of more than twenty million of his countrymen. Hitler exterminated six million Jews during the Holocaust and was responsible for the deaths of over seven million Germans during the war.

These two dictators initiated great tragedies and caused immense suffering in the world that lingers to this day. While World War Two has long been over there seems to be no end to tragedy and terror in the world. How many must die in the Mideast and elsewhere before people realize that peace, understanding, and cooperation are more important to life than hatred, rage, and retribution?

The terrible thing about rage and hatred is that once they gain a foothold in the mind of a people, the implacable thirst for vengeance follows quickly. Hatred blinds people to the possibility of finding common ground and moving toward a peaceful solution. In such an explosive situation clarity, objectivity, and compassion are the first casualties. When rage triumphs there is no space for dialogue, dissent, or common sense.

The goal of the dark side of human nature, and the tyrants and terrorists who are its champions, is to make sure that dialogue, dissent, and common sense do not occur in the general population. The dark side uses fear to create hatred and hatred to divert the population from its true interests - peace, security, and economic opportunity. The forces of darkness are too interested in being the ultimate authority to let a chance for peace get in the way of their hold on power.

Gandhi, in comparison, represented the power of light within hu man nature. He emancipated his people by placing their well-being before his own. Tyrants and terrorists do the opposite. That is why the Mahatma succeeded in his quest to free India and why the forces of darkness failed in their quest to conquer the world. The lessons of the past strongly suggest that tyranny and terrorism cannot endure. A people and a country can be subjugated for a time, but not for all time.

Serving a Higher Purpose

Gandhi was a highly moral person who was motivated by a higher purpose to serve his people. As he strove to free India from the yoke of the British Empire, that purpose accelerated his own growth and evolution. By dedicating his life to fulfilling that purpose Gandhi became a better man and a more conscious individual.

Since Gandhi had direct access to his soul, the manifestation of his true purpose brought a bright and hopeful light into the world. We should never underestimate the power of a true purpose. A person with a true purpose will elevate and enrich life. Christ, Buddha, Moses, Gandhi, and Mohammed started with nothing but the discovery of their true natures and their commitment to a higher purpose. What they each started still lives today. Each of them moved the mass culture forward and although they are all gone, their truths and teachings continue to enrich the lives of billions of people.

The Five Common Features of a True Purpose

All manifestations of a true purpose have five common features.

- *A true purpose is the result of Self-realization, of becoming who we were always meant to be.* The foundation of Self-realization is the merger of the conscious, rational mind with the soul.

⟿ *A true purpose is a form of unconditional love.*

⟿ *A true purpose serves and uplifts other people.*

⟿ *A true purpose creates acceptance among people and fosters group consciousness.*

⟿ *A true purpose encourages creativity and allows freedom to flourish.*

How Great Things Begin

Anyone who has the privilege of pursuing his true purpose realizes that when he fulfills his purpose, he also fulfills himself. Great things, even vast things, start in small ways with small actions that hardly register at the time. The beginning is often undetected until the purpose gathers momentum and attracts attention. The Roman Empire began over six hundred years before the birth of Christ with a small band of people in the Italian peninsula searching for a new home on a group of hills. That tiny blip on the screen of history became a great Empire that was to last a thousand years.

Christ began with a few followers in Judea, Buddha with a small band of disciples in India. Two millennia later, each of these great spiritual masters has a religion named after them and more than a billion followers.

Service and the Higher Light

The lives of Christ, Buddha, Mohammed, Gandhi, and the others demonstrate an important spiritual principle. If we move in the direction of serving a greater good than our own self-interest, the higher light of the spirit will support and protect our work. Our efforts to serve others will open the door to draw down a larger measure of Divine light. We don't have to free a country like Gandhi, found a religion like Christ and Mohammed, or discover the path to enlightenment as Buddha did. We only have to free ourselves from the chains within our psyche that bind us to our negative ego and desire nature.

Whenever one of us discovers his true self, another inner light goes on in the world. The more spiritual light that is present in the world,

31

the less that evil can live here. Our lives all count. We are all important. We each have a unique contribution to make that will allow the world to be a better place. Our identity and purpose are not only important for our own personal well-being, they are also important for the well-being of the world.

Forms of Service

A spiritual path can be compared to a snowflake. Like snowflakes, all paths are similar, but none are the same. There are as many ways to grow and serve, as there are people on the planet. The Divine is an equal opportunity employer who calls us all to His service. Serving the greater good requires a change of consciousness, an open heart, an attitude adjustment, and little more. It does not require a starched collar and a dark robe. We don't have to be ministers, priests, rabbis, nuns, monks, or imams. We don't have to leave our jobs. We just have to consider the well-being of others around us and be helpful to them when we have the opportunity to do so.

The Negative Ego

As long as the negative ego dominates our psyche, it will obscure our true identity and block us from our path. For however long this condition prevails, the negative ego will keep us bound entirely in selfish pursuits without any gratitude whatsoever for the sacrifices others may have made to help us achieve our goals. Sri Aurobindo commented on this condition when he wrote:

> The vital, (negative ego) is too selfish to have any gratitude. The more it gets, the more it demands, and it takes everything as its right and every denial of what it wants as an injustice and an offense.
>
> The unregenerate vital (negative ego) in the average human nature is not grateful for a benefit; it resents being under an obligation. So long as the benefit continues, it is effusive and says sweet things; as soon as it expects

nothing more it turns round and bites the hand that fed it. Sometimes it does that even before, when it thinks it can do it without the benefactor knowing the origin of the slander, fault finding, or abuse.*

Ignorance and apathy about who we really are discourage many people from seeking inner growth. Those among us whose world-view is largely shaped by material values and considerations often pay little attention to their non-physical needs. Frequently, what matters most is getting ahead in the world. Prestige, power, money, and status are what count. These are the things that are valued and prized. It's how most of us keep score and why we compete to get ahead of each other. As long as we get what we want in the world, what does the state of our soul really matter?

After all, we can't measure our internal light, compare it to others, compete for more of it, or place a monetary value on it. We can't buy it or sell it. It isn't a commodity. So if we can't prove that we have more light than everybody else, then why should we bother with the whole exercise?

Our Soul Asset

There is a profound reason why we should make that effort. Our conscious connection with our soul is the most important asset we will ever have. That connection must be developed here. It cannot be developed after we die. If we throw away our opportunities to develop our soul connection in this lifetime, we will not make the inner growth we came here to make or find a lasting fulfillment in our life. A major part of us will remain missing. A great resource that could successfully guide us through life's many challenges will remain untapped. Our true power and creativity will never be utilized. Our potential for happiness and inner peace will not be realized. If we fail to make our growth in this lifetime, it may make that task much harder in future lifetimes.

Since the purpose of life is to develop our soul connection, we never escape the pressure of that purpose. When we deny the most essential need of our nature, we unwittingly increase the hidden pressure of that

---

* Sri Aurobindo, *A Practical Guide to Yoga*, 163

purpose on our lives. That pressure may heighten our suffering, high-light our unhappiness, or widen our sense of alienation.

To the Divine, the most important factor in evaluating our life is the growth we made toward our soul. Did we turn on our light, find out who we really are, and make our unique contribution to the world? From the Divine perspective there is no more important task than this.

Siddhartha and Septimius

Siddhartha was a young prince in ancient India who walked away from ruling a kingdom, the love of a beautiful wife, the adoration of his people, and an opulent lifestyle that fulfilled all of his material needs to find that higher connection. He burned with an inner ferocity to find out who he really was. In the pursuit of his quest Siddhartha lived in forests, bathed in streams, wore a loincloth, journeyed from teacher to teacher, and ate whatever the forest would yield or people would give him. When he found his answer years later, he became Buddha, the enlightened one. Based on his Self-knowledge, Buddha realized that his purpose was to teach and share his knowledge of enlightenment.

Due to the strength and truth of his teachings, Buddha, the enlightened one, is more famous now than he ever would have been had he remained Siddhartha, the ruler of his people. If he had chosen the path of kingship, only a few obscure scholars would still know the name of Siddhartha, and no one would have ever heard of Buddha.

How many people today remember Septimius? In his lifetime, he had everything a person could desire. It did not fulfill him, nor did his fame last. His voice echoed for a short time then died. While Buddha has been dead for over two millennia, the noble truths he brilliantly articulated still guide the lives of countless millions.

In the end, only the truth matters. Self-realization is the real harvest of life. If we haven't found the truth of our being, what remains in our soul is the bitter darkness of our failure.

In the material world, fashions come and go. Trends change. What was once hot becomes cold, and what was long out of taste becomes sought after again. In contrast, the truth never changes. Somewhere, deep inside us all, we each have a hunger to find out who we really are. As human beings, we can't escape that hunger, no matter how cold, hard, distant, or unreachable we choose to make ourselves. We might bury our truth, deny it, and even try to disown it, but no matter what we do in our attempts to escape it, it will always be with us. It is a hunger that has been programmed into us as a species, one that has existed in all generations since the beginning of time. It is our deepest need and our most defining one.

The Connecting Point

The soul is the connecting point between our individual life and all other lives. It bridges the gap between the personality's emphasis on exclusion and separation, and the spirit's higher reality of inclusion and unity. While the personality focuses on our differences in order to create distance by making distinctions, the soul feels how we are subtly connected to each other and conspires to bring us together. Where the personality often breeds friction, the soul attempts to generate fusion.

The soul is the door to universal love. It draws the spiritual light down from above and distributes it to the world. It is the mediator between the Divine and the human, drawing the Divine to the human and the human to the Divine. When we finally open the door to our soul, we become a channel of unconditional love and a Divine ambassador in this world. Without us the Divine has limited means to enter the world and restore it to balance.

When we open ourselves up and allow the soul to gradually bring the light down from above, that light will slowly and surely elevate our lives. The soul enables us to understand and accept ourselves and then to understand and accept others. If we remain closed off to the soul, it seems that the Divine is unavailable and nowhere to be seen. When we successfully open ourselves to our soul, it is obvious and apparent that the Divine is everywhere.

When we develop access to our soul, we know it. It is not something that has to be proved. It is a force that guides and protects our life; a power of knowing that comes from deep inside us, a gift of inspired communication and heightened creativity. It is the magnetic force of a charisma that effortlessly attracts other people to it. It is an energy that inspires trust and initiates healing. It is an unconditional love in action that permits people to feel better about themselves, to conquer their self-doubt and confusion, and to extricate themselves from long cycles of suffering.

Our soul is our savior. Everyone has a soul, just as everyone has a heart and a brain, lungs and a liver. Yet for the most part, we hardly think about it. It is inactive in most of us, consigned to the background, hidden in the shadows.

Soul Resonance

The soul cannot communicate with us until, and unless, we are internally quiet and at peace. The constant chatter and internal dialogue that occurs in the minds of most people, most of the time, prevents that higher contact from taking place, but once we are centered and at peace, the gateway is opened and the ground prepared for that higher connection to occur. As our soul connection slowly develops, we are drawn to engage in activities that resonate with our soul.

The presence of soul resonance in our lives indicates a high probability of success and fulfillment in our endeavors. Soul resonance quickens the pace of our inner growth and personal evolution. While we need to find our way in the world we live in, we must also find our way within ourselves. To succeed in both tasks is rare, but need not be. Balance is the key to the future. Until we develop a strong soul connection, material success is attainable, but true fulfillment is always over the next hill. We have been educated to achieve and succeed. We must also learn to be clear, centered, and at peace. We have focused on training and developing our intellect. We now need to develop our intuition.

When we establish our soul connection, the world has more to gain from what we can give it than we have to gain from what the world can give us. The world has an abundance of most things, but it has a great shortage of wisdom, understanding, love, and compassion—all qualities of higher consciousness. If more of us developed soul resonance, we would find common ground more easily, and we would overcome conflict with less difficulty.

A change in mass consciousness is never easy, but to keep going in the direction we are now headed in is infinitely worse. It is far better to struggle for an improved future than to suffer a mass calamity because of our collective inertia.

The Soul, The Negative Ego, and Group Consciousness

Unlike the negative ego, the soul is not interested in exploiting other people for individual gain. Its agenda is not limited to the desires of the personality. It does not want to shine by shaming someone else. Its true interest lies in uplifting everyone so that we all might benefit. The soul's strategy is strongly focused on establishing group consciousness. Its game plan is straightforward. If we play together, we win together. If we heal together, we can change the world.

We cooperate with our soul's plan when we clear our karma and open the necessary space in our system for the soul to come forward and shine in our life. The soul is the door to unconditional love. Whenever unconditional love is present, everyone feels whole, uplifted, and empowered, the equal of everyone else in the group. Love is inclusive. Love makes winners of us all. Love changes the world.

The negative ego's game plan is quite different. Its strategies are divisive and center on this timeworn theme: If I win, you lose, and if you lose, then I get to feel better, bigger, and more important than you. The negative ego's game is devoid of unconditional love. It is full of hostility and exploitative maneuvers whose sole intention is to fulfill its desires, often shaming and humiliating other people for its own gains. The negative ego wants to dominate everyone and be at the top of the heap. It mistakenly thinks it can substitute "being on top" for being whole and fulfilled. What the negative ego fails to recognize is that being on top does not automatically make you whole, happy, or fulfilled. What you were before you got to the top of the heap, you will be after you get there. Power, wealth, and notoriety are not the antidote for having an empty core.

The Soul and the Long-term

The soul knows that it has had previous incarnations and may well have future ones. It knows that we come here, time and time again, until we learn the lessons that we must and transform the toxic energies we carry in our body into a clear and vibrant light. The soul's concern is for the long-term: Will what we do in this lifetime advance our long-term growth or hinder it?

Helping other people helps our growth. Kindness, forgiveness, and a generous spirit count. These qualities accelerate our growth and help us transmute whatever rage, resentment, and hatred we may experience within ourselves or encounter from others. Being stuck in negative emotion separates us from our soul, encumbers our progress, and holds us back.

The Negative Ego and the Short-term

Unlike the soul, the negative ego's concern is for the short-term, this lifetime. It has a short-term focus because that's all it thinks it has, one lifetime to get what it craves and then the grave. It wants to get everything it can in almost any way it can. It is ruled by desire and greed. It functions in ignorance of the Law of Consequence and has little, if any, consideration for the long-term repercussions of its actions. If death is the end of everything, thinks the negative ego, then what possible further consequences could there be for what I have done?

Ignorance however, is not a shield and will not protect the negative ego from the long-term consequences of its actions. Sooner or later those consequences will come home to roost. We never outwit or outrun the Law of Consequences.

Unlike the spirit which lives in clarity and peace, the negative ego lives in constant worry. Because it feels separate and alone, fear is never far away. It is the first emotion the negative ego feels when it faces the unknown. The spirit, on the other hand, has a conscious realization of its own eternal continuity. It is centered in the Divine light. The real challenge of life is to find that center.

three The Three Zones Of Personal Evolution

*To change, a person must face the dragon of his appetites
with another dragon, the life energy of the soul.*

Rumi

*There's no point to proving your superiority over
another person but a lot to be gained by being superior
to your former self.*

Old Indian Proverb

*Life is suffering. The root of suffering is desire. To
eliminate suffering one must eliminate desire.*

The Buddha

There are three zones involved in the process of opening up our system to the soul. Taken together, these three zones comprise the path of personal evolution. If we fulfill the requirements of these three zones, we will realize our potential. In the first zone on the path of personal evolution, our primary work is to overcome past karma and clear unconscious emotional toxicity from our system. In the second zone, our main work is to stand up for ourselves, integrate our nature, and find our wholeness. In the third zone, our central task is to discover who we really are and fulfill our life purpose. The tasks we need to master in these three zones are sequential in nature, and if we are to succeed in this work, these steps must be taken in their correct order. To approach them out of sequence is to guarantee failure. The three zones of the path of personal evolution in their correct order of sequence are:

    ⊸   *The Elimination Zone*

    ⊸   *The Integration Zone*

    ⊸   *The Elevation Zone*

The Three Ego Levels

Each of these three zones also has a corresponding level of ego associated with it. In the Elimination Zone, we have to contend with the resistant and obstructive nature of the negative ego. The negative ego has no interest in moving forward because its sole interest is in maintaining its control over our entire system.

In the Integration Zone, the negative ego has been transformed and emerges as the healthy ego. The healthy ego seeks to move in harmony with the soul and spirit. Its primary values are growth and freedom rather than control and repression. It is committed to moving forward.

In the Elevation Zone, the healthy ego gives way to the surrendered ego. The surrendered ego has fused with the soul and spirit, becoming their ally and their door to the world. In the third stage of personal evolution, there is no more tension or conflict between the ego and the higher dimensions of our being. A deep peace and clarity settles over the entire nature. The differences in these ego states, as well as their potential transformations, will be discussed in greater detail in later chapters.

The Elimination Zone

The Elimination Zone is where we must start. The central focus of the Elimination Zone is clearing the toxic, incomplete emotional experiences that we have buried in our body and failed to face. Virtually everyone has this kind of toxicity imbedded in his body, but for the most part, we are unaware of the existence of much of this material.

Let's consider the imaginary case of an adult male who grew up in a family with unstable, alcoholic parents. As a young child, our young man never felt safe enough to express his emotions or to ask for what he needed. He received little nurturing, approval, or love from his parents. When he got home from school he never knew what conditions awaited him. Would his mother scream at him? Would his father beat him? Would there be food for dinner?

His childhood was an ongoing nightmare. He was preoccupied with conditions that another child, growing up in a stable and loving home, would never have to face. He had nowhere to turn and no one to confide in. There was no safe harbor in his life, no way to reduce the pressures he had to confront everyday. He was alone in the horror of his childhood.

His solution for dealing with the exigencies of his life was to take the only path available to him, which I have named the path of most resistance. As he trudged down this path he learned to shut off his feelings and numb his system to the constant assaults he faced from his parents. Not feeling was the only way he had to endure and survive.

Shutting Down and Surviving

When there is no one to protect a young child, the only way that child can protect himself from further psychological harm is to shut down emotionally. Shutting down is not really a conscious choice, but is rather an unconscious mechanism to stop the emotional bleeding. Turning off the ability to feel will shut off the pain and silence the inevitable rage, at least part of the time. Unfortunately, it also means that the person who shuts down his feelings has lost his ability to feel and, therefore, to connect with other people in any meaningful way. Instead of feeling connected to his world, he will feel empty, alone, alienated from those around him, and dead inside. In shutting down emotionally he also severs his connection to his soul.

While shutting down his ability to feel allows him to survive, that protection comes at a high cost. In addition to feeling empty, he has also made himself into a chronic victim: powerless, unbalanced, and angry. The chronic inner victim will not magically disappear when his childhood ends and he tries to make his way in the world. Instead, the inner victim will continue to undermine him and make his life a living hell. He will be his own worst enemy. This is the path of most resistance.

The strategy that enabled him to survive his childhood then may well poison his adulthood. By burying his pain instead of facing it, he increases the odds that he will duplicate his parent's dysfunction and like them, become a tortured soul laden with toxic shame. If he becomes a parent one day, without first healing his childhood nightmare, it is highly likely that he will do to his own children what his parents did to him.

In essence, when a parental dysfunction penetrates the subconscious of a child, that dysfunction is passed on from the older generation to the younger one and will persist as a dominant family behavior until someone in the family decides to confront and eliminate it in himself. If the children do not eliminate it when they become adults, it will be passed on to their children. If that toxicity remains firmly entrenched in the subconscious of family members, it can persist for many generations. As it passes down through the generations, it may also become more virulent with each new replication.

When a child shuts down emotionally, there are serious repercussions in the rest of his life. What he shuts down will be difficult to open later. Whenever someone shuts himself down, he locks a strong sense of his worthlessness and shame deep within his core. He will feel that he can never redeem himself, no matter what he does. It's not that he has made mistakes in his life that he can atone for, as much as it seems to him that his whole life has been a mistake. How does he atone for that? Since that shame is who he mistakenly thinks he is, he may resist facing it with great ferocity. After all, he feels unredeemable. Facing the pain at the core of his psyche is like facing his death.

As time passes, and he attempts to move forward, his imbedded shame will become the shame of which he is no longer even conscious. It will imprison him in the alienation and emptiness of the past and prevent him from finding wholeness and happiness in the present. If he marries and has children, his unconscious shame will be his legacy to the next generation.

The Cycle of Adult Shame

The adult cycle of our young man's imbedded shame begins with his denial that he was invalidated and made to feel worthless as a child. That conscious denial strengthens his unconscious shame and guarantees that he will continue to endure a sense of worthlessness that will gnaw at him incessantly. He will bear a strong sense of inferiority that nothing he achieves can overcome for long.

The same shame that exists in our young man exists in many of us. Those feelings don't go away with time or disappear with our denial. They don't melt away because we wish them too. In fact, the more we ignore them and pretend they don't exist, the louder and more powerful they become. The more they penetrate our subconscious, the more they control our life. The unconscious shame we try to deaden in our system then, is not really dead at all.

If buried and unacknowledged shame is present in our subconscious, it will determine much of what happens in our lives. Whatever that shame brings into our lives will be detrimental to our well-being. Our unacknowledged shame will deprive us of our true identity and fulfillment and prevent us from integrating the physical and non-physical elements of our system. It will keep us from being whole and balanced. This is the legacy of the path of most resistance.

Making matters worse, when toxic shame is present in our subconscious, our ego has a negative orientation. A major function of the negative ego is to keep us from finding and confronting that buried shame. Its job is to keep our shame unconscious. Its mission is to keep shame alive. The only real solution to dealing with unconscious shame is to make it conscious. However, when the ego is negative it will do everything it can to keep that shame buried and unconscious.

Surviving life with toxic shame embedded in our system is far from living life without it. We can survive, we can endure, but until we clear the toxic emotion buried in our bodies, we cannot go forward. We will not find our purpose, our happiness, our freedom, or ourselves. We will just survive and endure, feeling worthless and unredeemable, living life without being fully alive.

For our adult child of alcoholic parents to go forward, he will have to face, feel, and complete all the painful, incomplete, and toxic emotion stored in his body. He will have to confront his shame, his feelings of worthlessness, and his unending sense of emptiness. This, of course, takes courage. It will not be easy for him to be vulnerable to the parts of his nature that he thinks are unredeemable. That's why he erected a negatively oriented ego in the first place. However, there is a way out. If he chooses to face and feel his toxic emotions he can complete them. When he finally completes those emotions they will be discharged from his system. He will then stand clear of his past, and be well on his way to wholeness and happiness. If, however, he chooses the path of most resistance and decides to avoid facing his toxicity, his situation will not improve.

Almost all of us have our own incomplete emotion and unconscious shame to deal with. We may not have had alcoholic parents like our imaginary young man did, but virtually all of us have some dysfunction or disturbance to clear from our system that keeps us from being whole and integrated, in touch with our true identity, and able to manifest our true purpose.

Elimination is an exacting, demanding, and often exhausting process. The more shame and emotional toxicity we carry in our system, the further away from ourselves we are. Hopefully, our young man will get so tired of the way he is living that he will be willing to face his toxicity at last. If he can turn away from the path of most resistance, where he is constantly running from himself, and enter the path of personal evolution, where he chooses to face himself, he will be able to find his way home to who he really is.

The Seven Principles of Negative Force

There are seven principles of negative force that exert constant pressure on us. If we don't eliminate the incomplete, toxic emotion from our system, these principles become the power in our lives. They limit our growth and keep us from finding happiness.

The refusal to face the past guarantees its continued presence in our lives. The failure to face what once happened assures that it will repeat itself many times, in many guises, until we finally choose to confront it.

Over five thousand years ago, Lao Tzu, the founder of Taoism, shared this insight about dealing with inner obstacles: "Because the sage confronts his difficulties, he never experiences them." The wise man never postpones the moment of reckoning. When he confronts his difficulties as they arise, no toxic shadow remains from the past to follow him into the future. No ancient blight waits in hiding, only to arise as if from nowhere, to poison his life.

The seven principles of negative force that control our lives until we eliminate our toxicity are as follows:

- *Whatever we fail to confront steals our power and diminishes us.*

- *Whatever we avoid or deny controls us.*

- *Whatever controls us keeps us from standing in our own power.*

- *Whatever keeps us from standing in our power keeps us from realizing our true self.*

- *Whatever keeps us from realizing our true self keeps us from actualizing our purpose.*

- *Whatever keeps us from actualizing our purpose keeps us from freedom and fulfillment.*

- *There is no time limit on the hidden toxicity of the past. It does not have an expiration date and will not disappear on its own.*

If we don't take action to defeat our toxicity, it will easily defeat us. It does not lose its power to affect us adversely until we clear it. Clearing our emotional toxicity is absolutely necessary if we are to stand in our power and discover who we really are.

Death and Continuity

Death is no obstacle to the continuation of unresolved toxic content. If we fail to clear a toxic condition during the lifetime in which it occurred, that toxic event is stored as a packet of blocked and polluted energy in our soul. When we incarnate again in another life, the toxic conditions in our soul will return with us. In our next lifetime we may have a different personality, a new look, and a new focus, but we will have the same heavy burden to carry that we inherited from our last lifetime. While everything else may be different about us, our soul, and the karma it carries, will be the same.

The unhealed wounds from our past life will continue to live inside us, unknown and unheeded. The fact that they are now completely unknown makes them more difficult to overcome. When the unhealed wounds of the past travel with us to a new lifetime, they attain a quality of *invisibility* that compounds the problems we face in finding them. Their invisibility gives them a deep cover. While we can access our past experiences in this lifetime fairly easily, we don't normally have access to our *soul history* from past incarnations.

Revelation and Redemption

It takes a very bright and powerful light to penetrate deeply enough into our system to reveal these lost, long forgotten, and troubled fragments of our experience. These pieces must be revealed before they can be redeemed. The revelation of our hidden toxicity requires the *descent* of a higher spiritual light into the depths of our subconscious. That light will reveal what has long been hidden.

The redemption of our hidden wounds requires the *ascent* of these toxic emotions into the light of consciousness, where they can be faced, felt, and cleared. Only then is the past redeemed and our system cleared of its encumbrances.

If we do not heal our wounds, they will continue bleeding, robbing us of our power to be whole. Our wounds block our evolution. They place shadows of fear across our minds. They are the unseen chains that bind us to old agonies and prevent us from moving forward into a better and more fulfilling life. The most powerful and direct way to access these wounds is to focus the higher light of the spirit on the subconscious with laser-like precision and drive these experiences from the darkness in which they reside.

The Power of Choice

Everything that we have not yet worked out of our system must be worked out eventually, either in this life or a future one. The longer we delay that task, the more we prolong our unhappiness. The *only* power we have over our buried toxicity is the power of choosing when to face it. The sooner we choose to face our unresolved trauma, the easier it is to re-solve the emotional blocks that hold us back. When toxic energy is close to the surface, it is easy to find and bring to our conscious mind. But if we postpone our confrontation with the toxic events that are lodged in our system, we unwittingly provide those events with the opportunity to burrow even more deeply into our body. If we don't seize the opportu-nity to clear toxic material from our system as soon as we can, that tox-icity will seize its opportunity to run as far as it can from our conscious mind. Our toxicity seeks to conceal what we need to reveal in order to regain our balance and accelerate our evolution. By hiding what should be exposed the negative ego maintains its control over our psyche.

If our toxicity remains concealed, our personal power will remain bound up with what has wounded us, and continues to wound us still. When our wounds control us, we have little power. We become more powerless and unhappy with each new wound. Because we lack access to our real power, the focus of our future won't be found in fulfilling our destiny, but rather in repeating our drudgery. The legacy of failing to act is a lifetime of failure.

DONALD

Every lifetime has its moment of truth. We can step into the great un-known and seize our destiny, or we can grasp our fear more tightly and sink deeper into our darkness. Donald is a musician from Oregon who heard me being interviewed on a nationally syndicated late night radio show. He had been drowning in his pain for many years. During those years, he had tried many different therapies and popular seminars with-out success. He was desperate to resolve his suffering, and what he heard me say that night gave him the courage to roll the dice one more time.

Donald decided to come to a three-day training I held in Los

Angeles. During the first two days of the training he felt some anger and fear coming up when it was his time to be worked on, but it was nothing like what he had hoped would happen for him. On the third day of the training I made it to his table and worked with him for nearly an hour. When we started, I placed one of my hands under his tailbone and the other on top of his abdomen. As I put my hands on his body, I saw pictures in my mind of an American P.O.W. from World War Two being tortured by Japanese soldiers. I told Donald what I was seeing. My perceptions touched a deep nerve within him, and the hidden emotional toxicity that he had been trying to reach for years came surging to the surface. For the next hour Donald writhed, screamed, and twisted his body all over the table as he relived the trauma from that lifetime and cleared the toxicity from his system. When he finished clearing that layer of toxicity, he lay resting on the table, his body at peace, his eyes bright, and his face luminous. He laughed and joked and gave everyone in his group a big hug.

While I had only told Donald the barest outlines of what I had seen at the beginning of his session, it had been enough to trigger the release of toxic emotion that he had so desperately needed. Although he felt unfulfilled by the two previous days of work my words would have been useless without those two days of preparation. The healing energy in the seminar room worked on him from the first day to the time we ended on the third day. It never stopped working on him, even while he ate and slept. During those few days, the healing energy accomplished its mission. It mobilized his toxic material and brought it close to the surface where not only I could see it, but also where he finally could find it, face it, feel it, and clear it.

Some months later I received a letter from Donald. He wrote that, "I feel so different. I don't hear that nagging voice I used to hear in my head. It's just not there anymore. I feel so much peace within and it's so much easier to look at other people. I just don't feel that fear anymore. All things considered, I just feel so much better about everything."

While we might be afraid to know and feel what lies beneath the surface of our conscious mind, the actual confrontation with that buried material is not nearly as painful or scary as it might seem. In fact, it is more of a relief than anything else. When it is over, we feel lighter in body, mind, and soul.

KAREN

Some years before the Los Angeles training, I gave a seminar in Virginia. Among the people in attendance that afternoon was a woman sitting near the front of the room who seemed very uncomfortable in her own skin. As I looked more closely at her from a clairvoyant perspective, I saw that the traumatic events of her last lifetime were visible in her aura. She had died horribly in the Holocaust, burned to death in the furnaces of a concentration camp.

I began the seminar and talked for a while, but my attention kept being drawn to her. I could see that her unconscious toxicity was ready to "pop" and that her inner being had led her to this seminar so that she could clear those buried events from her system. I could further see that the manner of her death in her last lifetime had cast a long shadow of fear and terror over her present life and that she knew none of this consciously.

Finally, I couldn't bear her pain anymore. I felt that part of my assignment that day was to free her from her unconscious toxicity. So I did the only thing I could think to do. I asked her if she would come up front and lie down on the healing table next to me so I could demonstrate how the healing process worked.

She looked all around her, terrified of being singled out and separated from her friends. "Why me?" she asked.

"Because you're ready, and I think you'll be a very good subject."

"I don't feel ready."

"That's to be expected. People who are ready are in touch with their fear. Your high level of anxiety just means you're really ready."

"Well, I'm not so sure of that."

"I understand. Nobody is ever very sure of anything when they are really ready to let go. It sort of feels like the rug is being pulled out from under you and everything in your life is suddenly being turned upside down. But all we're going to do here is find what you're ready to let go of and then discharge it. So if you can be a bit brave and take a risk, everything will be fine."

"But…"

"I'll tell you what. If you feel very uncomfortable at any point in the process, we'll stop."

"Really?"

"Really."

Having a way out convinced her to give it a try. She came up and hesitantly got on the table. I put one hand under the base of her spine, and my other hand under the base of her skull. The energy immediately started flowing out of me into her central nervous system. As I watched the energy flow into her, it surrounded her body with bands of green, blue, gold, and white energy. I could see that the audience was feeling the energy as well. Their restlessness faded away. They became quiet, peaceful, and alert. Within two to three minutes I could tell that Karen was very relaxed. Her eyes closed; her breathing became slow and even. I now moved my hands to her abdomen and her left side where the toxic energy of that terrible death was stored. As I shifted my hands, the healing energy flowing from my hands also shifted. It was now a bright, fiery red. Within seconds of the energy shifting, Karen opened her eyes and stared at me in shock.

"It's Okay," I said softly, so only she could hear. "Some old stuff from your last life is ready to pop. Just make a little sound and it will come pouring out of you."

"What stuff?" she asked, terrified.

I had no chance to respond. With those two words her repressed material came flooding out. She started to cry. Her body shook. She waved her arms and legs frantically, wailed and screamed. After twenty minutes of intense release, her physical movements stopped. Her body became quiet as her system filled with peace. As she shifted from one state of consciousness to another, from a state of cathartic healing to a state of deep peace, the energy going into her changed once more from bright red to pink, lavender, and gold.

I looked out at the audience. The faces in front of me registered fear and terror.

"I bet you're all afraid of getting on the table now."

They all nodded nervously.

"Looks pretty dangerous and painful, huh?"

They all nodded again. By this time Karen was back from her experience and had opened her eyes.

"Karen, could you tell the people in the audience how you feel?"

"I feel really great. I have never felt as light and peaceful as I feel now."

"Was it scary and painful to go through that release?"

"Not at all. I thought it would be, but it wasn't. Instead, all I could feel was a great sense of relief. I know it probably didn't look like that, but that is how it felt. It was funny too because once it started happening, I didn't have any control over it. It just sort of gushed out of me."

"Did you see any visions or have any insights during the experience?"

"I just felt like I was being burned alive."

"Were you afraid?"

"I experienced a brief moment of absolute terror in the beginning, just before that feeling surfaced, but once the feeling of being burned alive surfaced, the sense of terror faded away."

"Are you still afraid?"

"No. That's what's amazing. The fear is completely gone. I feel much lighter than I ever have. What did you see that made you call me up here?"

"I saw that you had been burned to death in your last lifetime, as you correctly felt you had. It was during the Holocaust, and you were incinerated in a concentration camp. That experience was very close to the surface of your being and was ready to be cleared. That's why I wanted you up here. Frankly, it was driving me a bit crazy, and I knew I had to clear it for you before we could go on with the seminar. I believe you were here today to clear it. How do you react when you see World War Two movies or read about the Holocaust?"

"I've never been able to watch anything to do with World War Two or even think about the Holocaust. The thought of it has always tied me up in fear and made me nauseous. Now I know why."

"It's always helpful to connect the dots and know why. It's even better to be free of what has held you back."

Every time we clear a toxic event from our psyche, we wrest more control and territory away from the negative ego. Each time we clear a toxic event, we expand our light, deepen our inner peace, bring our soul and conscious mind closer to each other, and lead our whole system closer to integration. Facing what we fear and going through some discomfort is a small price to pay for the freedom to evolve without internal resistance and the joy of becoming the person we were always meant to be.

four THE FOUR CATEGORIES

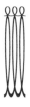

*You have to do your own growing no matter how tall
your grandfather was.*
Abraham Lincoln

I'm a slow walker, but I never walk back.
Abraham Lincoln

The degree to which our toxicity is mobile determines how easy or difficult it will be to resolve our buried trauma. In working with thousands
of clients over a period of more than twenty years, I have found that
people fall into four main categories. All four categories are defined by
two critical factors. The first critical factor is the quality of our unconscious toxicity. That toxicity is either mobile and ready to shift, or rock-
like and too entrenched to move. The second factor is the strength and
durability of our conscious intention to heal our lives.

In a category one client, the unconscious, toxic content is mobile
and ready to move. The client's conscious mind is also focused on healing and integration. In a category one client, both subconscious and conscious readiness is high. The internal context is in agreement. Since both
critical factors to the transformational process are in rapport with each
other, the internal distance that must be closed between the category one
client's unconscious toxic content and his conscious acknowledgement
of that content is minimal. The shorter that internal distance, the faster
the transformational process can proceed.

In a category two client, the unconscious, toxic content is as mobile
as it is in a category one client. However, the category two client's conscious mind has little interest in healing and integration. In a category two

client, subconscious readiness remains high, but conscious readiness is low. The internal context is therefore in conflict. There is less rapport between the subconscious and conscious minds than in a category one client. Despite the internal conflict that exists between the readiness of the subconscious to transform the toxicity it contains and the unwillingness of the conscious mind to participate in that transformational process, the degree of internal distance separating the client's toxicity from his conscious acceptance of that toxicity remains minimal.

Internal distance is created by the degree of mobility or lack of mobility in one's unconscious toxicity. The internal distance is minimal when one's toxicity is mobile and much more significant when one's toxicity is rock like. When the client's conscious resistance is overcome, the category two client becomes a category one. In most cases, overcoming that resistance is fairly simple, and the transformation of unconscious toxicity happens rapidly.

In a category three client, the relationship of the subconscious to the conscious mind is reversed. The category three client is the opposite of the category two client. The unconscious, toxic content in his subconscious is no longer mobile. It is immobile, rock-like, and not yet ready to move. His conscious mind, on the other hand, is now focused on healing and integration. The subconscious readiness of the category three client is low, while his conscious intention is high. The internal context of the category three client is in conflict, although for exactly the opposite reason of the category two client.

The category three client's unconscious toxicity is not yet ready to be transformed. Due to the lack of mobility in his toxic content, the internal distance separating the category three client's unconscious toxicity from his conscious experience of that toxicity is significant. Because of the rock-like nature of his unconscious toxicity, the task facing the category three client is more formidable than the task facing the category two. Overcoming that distance and mobilizing his toxic content will take time and persistence.

In the case of the category three client, his conscious intention is the paramount variable in his success or failure. If he is persistent, he will eventually succeed. If he isn't, he will become discouraged and fail. When the category three client's subconscious resistance has been mobilized, he too will become a category one.

In a category four client, the unconscious content is immobile and unready to move, and the conscious mind has no interest in healing and integration. In a category four, the readiness of both the subconscious and conscious mind is low. No aspect of the psyche is interested in or ready to be transformed. The intention to grow and evolve does not yet exist. Like the category one client, the internal context of the category four client is in agreement. The subconscious mind and conscious mind again are in rapport. However, unlike the category one client, the category four client's internal agreement is about keeping out the light and maintaining the negative conditions in the psyche. The category four individual has absolutely no interest in transformation at any level and, therefore, is not ready to transform himself into a category one client.

A category one client is a pleasure to work with. He wants to move forward and is ready to move forward. His conscious intention is matched by his subconscious readiness. His growth is rapid.

In dealing with a category two client, the trick is to overcome his conscious resistance. The good news for the category two client is that while he may not consciously have an interest in healing himself, he is fully ready to transform his life on a deeper level. He just don't know it until that healing happens.

A category three client is much more difficult and challenging to work with than either of the prior two categories. The reason for the added degree of difficulty in working with a category three is that the subconscious toxicity in his system is immobile. A category three thinks he is ready to transform his life, but the reality is that he is not as ready to transform his life as he thinks he is. The gap between expectation and reality often leads to frustration on his part because he cannot transform his life as quickly as he wants to. The whole trick in working with the category three client is to mobilize his toxicity. For a category three individual to succeed, his conscious intent must be stronger than his subconscious resistance.

A category three client will succeed if he lets go of his expectations, accepts the state of his toxicity for what it is, is persistent in confronting it, and patient with the pace of his progress. It has been my experience in working with category threes that the end result always justifies the time, work, and energy that goes into mobilizing their unconscious toxicity. The category three client should keep in mind that anything worth achieving is worth the effort that it takes to get there. If he doesn't expect the work to go quickly and easily, he won't be disappointed. He should not succumb to discouragement but should remember that the subconscious does not always yield its secrets on first demand, as it does in the case of a category one or two client.

By chipping away at his toxicity on a daily basis, the category three client will slowly take his power back from his unconscious trauma and karma. For the category three, the journey may be frustrating and longer than desired, but that will only make the journey's end sweeter than imagined. A more inclusive consciousness may be difficult to attain but is always worth the struggle it takes to get there. In the end, we appreciate more that which we must struggle to attain than that which comes to us easily. When we have to struggle to grow, we learn the true price of personal freedom.

I myself was a category three. Even after many years of healing other people, reaching the deepest levels of my own toxicity proved to be very challenging. The unconscious content remaining in my system had very little mobility. A strong conscious effort on my part was required to defeat an equally strong subconscious resistance.

In my case, I had already cleared most of the toxicity from my present lifetime. Mobilizing the deeply entrenched and hidden toxicity from several past lifetimes was the hard part. It took many months of hard work and persistent effort to mobilize that material. However, when those events were finally mobilized, they proved easy to clear. When I processed those ancient experiences, many regions of blocked energy cleared out along my spine. I became more limber and my chronic low back pain disappeared.

During this period I experienced lifetimes in which I had been drawn and quartered, put in an iron vest that had hundreds of long, sharp spikes pointed inward toward the body and pierced my chest, ribs, heart and lungs as the vest was tightened and I died a slow, and terrible death. I fought and died in battle as a Native American warrior and lost my mother tragically as a young boy in medieval Spain, and that was just a little bit of what came out of me. It was enervating to go through these events but tremendously rewarding at the same time to have done so. The rewards far exceeded the cost of clearing them from my system.

In the case of a category three client, conscious intention makes all the difference. In fact, conscious persistence in the face of unconscious adversity deflates the power of our wounds to wound us further.

In retrospect, it served me well to have had to go through a period of struggle and frustration before I achieved the mobility I needed to clear my toxicity. That period of struggle helped me in two ways. First, it made my toxicity even more mobile than would have been the case if that toxicity had been naturally fluid. Second, it made even deeper levels of toxicity available for processing.

When certain levels of a person's toxicity are naturally mobile, it does not follow that all levels of that person's toxicity will also be mobile. In most cases, there are deeper levels of toxicity hidden beneath the more mobile ones. These deeper layers are like bedrock and often lay embedded and undetected in the darkest regions of the psyche. Since they often originate in traumatic experiences from other lifetimes, we no longer have a direct conscious connection to them and no longer remember them. As a result, the internal distance we must travel to find them may be quite formidable.

These embedded and undetected events are unaffected by the layers above them, just like the depths of the ocean are unaffected by whatever movements may be occurring in the regions closer to the surface. These deeper layers of toxicity do not yield their secrets easily. It takes work to discover them and a high degree of conscious intention to clear them. When we do clear them, however, the power they have to repeat and reconfigure themselves in our lives dies with them.

We know we have really reached mobility when the toxic material takes over and pours out of us. At that point we are no longer in conscious control, and the negative ego rapidly loses its power to dominate our lives. A revolution in the psyche is underway. From that point on, we won't have to struggle to find our toxicity. We have crossed the internal distance we must travel to reach that toxicity. We are now reconfiguring the dynamics of our psyche and revolting against the repressive regime of the negative ego. We are knocking on the door to freedom, awakening to the light in the core of our being. We are being reborn and we will never be the same.

five THE FORCES OF ALIENATION

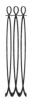

Where love rules there is no will to power and where
power predominates there love is lacking. The one is the
shadow of the other.

Carl Gustaf Jung

The opposite of success is generosity; the opposite of
recognition is service; the opposite of power and status
are loving relationships. We have enough of greed and
success. You become an adult when you realize you are
not here to get, you're here to give.

Kenneth Blanchard, L.A. Times Oct. 16,2002

The Three Forces of Alienation

Whenever the negative ego rules the psyche, the three forces of alienation — fear, greed, and desire — will dominate our emotional landscape
and determine much of our behavior. We fall into fear when we fall out
of the light. The price we pay for falling into fear is the increased separation of our conscious mind from our soul and spirit. In separating us
from our soul and spirit, fear also separates us from unconditional love.
When we lose our ability to love unconditionally greed and desire become the dominant motivational forces in the psyche.

While the expression of unconditional love leads to inner fulfillment
and joy, the chronic expression of greed and desire leads to frustration
and an ever-deeper feeling of emptiness. Where unconditional love elevates and expands our consciousness, bringing us closer to our soul and
spirit, greed and desire have the opposite effect. They contract our awareness and widen the gap between our conscious mind and our soul.

Greed and desire are fear's children. The more we pursue the ob–
jects of our greed and desire, the farther away from our true nature
those pursuits will take us. The farther we travel from our true nature,
the more inauthentic we become. As our disingenuousness increases,
our fear proliferates. Fear is a closed circuit that leads through greed and
desire and back again to fear. Every time we complete that circuit, our
fear grows stronger and becomes more entrenched in our system. The
stronger our fear becomes, the more powerful our attachment grows
to greed and desire. As the three forces of alienation grow within us, we
downgrade the importance of unconditional love and mock the reality
of the soul and spirit. We then mistake our state of separation as our ultimate reality. When we buy into the belief of separation, we invest our
energy in life's great illusion.

Alienation

Alienation occurs when the physical and supra-physical aspects of our
system are separated from each other and prevented from working together. Fear, greed, and desire keep the two major aspects of our system
not only separate and divided, but also in conflict with each other as well.
The more we permit the three forces of alienation to run rampant in our
psyches, the more difficult it will be to find our true identity. When we
are divided internally, it is easy to be in conflict and extremely difficult
to be at peace.

Our world is a product of our internal alienation. Through that
alienation we have created a world rife with conflict of all sorts and on
all levels. It is a world that has too much violence and too little peace.
If we can't find peace within ourselves, how can we expect the world to
provide that peace for us? The world is not responsible for our well-being. Quite to the contrary, we are collectively responsible for the world's
well-being. Unfortunately, because of the pervasive problem of alienation from the spirit and soul that plagues humanity, as well as the selfishness that alienation habitually breeds, we typically fail to consider
the ramifications of our behavior on the world in which we live until it
is too late.

The Foundation of Higher Consciousness

A peaceful nature has always been the foundation of higher consciousness. As long as we are alienated from ourselves we cannot be at peace, and we will find it impossible to complete ourselves, move forward into the light, and elevate our lives. When we are only aware of part of ourselves, we cannot know who we really are. The problem of alienation is not only universal but is also the source of the silent epidemic of imbalance now plaguing the world. When we are alienated from ourselves, our spirit and our soul are absent from our lives. Without their influence, we can neither be in balance nor in tune with a reality larger than our own selfish interests. If we are not in touch with a larger reality, we will lack a cohesive and integrative vision to guide our lives, and without that vision we will be unable to find our purpose. Gandhi, Mother Teresa, Nelson Mandela, and the Dalai Lama, for instance, all had a coherent vision with a common theme. That common theme was serving the greater good of their people. Those visions were unselfish and motivated by unconditional love.

When the spirit is active in our lives, we can find common ground and resolve our differences. However, when the spirit is absent from our lives, those same differences quickly become insurmountable. In the aggregate, the three forces of alienation promote the increasing escalation of conflict and polarization throughout the world. They affect the individual by keeping him stirred up and focused on ambitions that do not serve his higher nature or allow him to fulfill himself but that lead him, instead, farther from inner peace and personal fulfillment.

The King and His Son

There is a wonderful story from the Old Testament that concerns a family conflict between a king and his son and the power of the spirit to resolve that conflict. The king had been preoccupied with matters of state and unable to spend much time with his family. One day, he decided he wanted to see his son so he called in his chief minister and instructed him to find the young man and bring him to his audience chamber at once. After a long search the minister found the son and told him of the king's order. The young man said he was busy at the moment and couldn't come to the palace to see his father. The chief minister was appalled. In his world you didn't defy the orders of a king. However, since he had no power to force the king's son to return to the palace, the chief minister had no choice but to return empty handed and report to the king what the young prince had said. The king was shocked and upset when the chief minister told him his son's answer. After all he was the king. No one dared to disobey him. Who was his son to do so?

Again he ordered his chief minister to find the young man and command him to come to the palace immediately. The chief minister, however, could not find the young man. Eventually, he learned that king's son had fled the kingdom. With a heavy heart the chief minister returned to the palace and informed the king that his son had run away. This time instead of getting angry, the king became introspective and quiet. The father in him took over. As he thought the matter through, he realized that his relationship with his son was far more important than his authority and control over him. His insensitive demands had driven his son away. Only his love and respect could bring him back. With his mind now clear, the king gave new instructions to his chief minister, "Go and find my son, and when you have found him, tell him to come as far as he can. I will come the rest of the way."

The possibility of losing his son had shocked the king and brought him back to his true nature. By moving outside his ego, he connected with his soul and found the answer to his problem. By stepping outside his role as the king, and away from his power to dominate the lives of his subjects that this role gave him, he was able to act with humility and find common ground with his son. By placing a more important value on serving his son than on controlling him, the king displayed his wisdom.

We are not always as wise as the king or as prepared to be humble in the service of love and truth. Instead of moving back a step, cooling down, and seeking to find the way out of conflict, we are often prone to react under the auspices of the three forces of alienation, fear, greed, and desire, thereby making things much worse for everyone involved, including ourselves.

Emptiness and Futility

Whenever the three forces of alienation attain systemic dominance in our lives, the end result of that dominance is a growing conviction of the futility of life. If we are busy and successful we can override that sense of futility for a time, but our success will never entirely eradicate it. We can cover it up, but we cannot expunge it.

Most people make the mistake of thinking that if they succeed in the external world, their success will automatically translate to their inner life: that in some mysterious, mystical, unthinking, and unfathomable fashion, their affluence will cross-pollinate and blossom into happiness, meaning, peace, and fulfillment. The long history of man, however, suggests a far different outcome. Cross-pollination has always been far more a hope than it ever has been a reality. While mankind has renewed its pursuit of this dream in each successive generation, spiritual law suggests that in doing so we have put the cart before the horse. What we gain in the world does not translate into increased internal light, nor can it compensate for what we lose when we ignore our inner growth. However, if we were to reverse the normal order of things and seek our growth first, success would come to us in a much easier fashion, and that success would be more in harmony with our essential nature. When we find ourselves, it is much easier to be fulfilled than it is to attempt to find fulfillment when we don't yet know who we are.

The Subtle Trap of Success

Becoming successful, without becoming aware of who we really are, may present a clear and present danger to our internal balance and well-being. As our degree of success increases, we may think that the darkness at the core of our being is irrelevant, or alternatively, we may believe that we don't have any toxicity to deal with. But dismissing the effect of that toxicity on our lives, or denying its existence, does not mean that we have deactivated it. That toxicity is still alive deep inside us, watching and waiting, luxuriating in our denial of its existence, biding its time, attracting scant attention, building its force and making its plans, all the while lulling us into thinking that it is no longer a threat.

It is always a threat. It will strike when it is ready and we are not. It will appear on its schedule and with its own agenda, one that is certain to be in conflict with ours. It will come when it has all the advantages and we have none. It will throw us off balance, and it will most assuredly wreak more havoc in our lives. Of course, when that toxicity surfaces, the most likely way that we will react to its appearance is by unleashing the three forces of alienation in an attempt to control the damage to our lives. In following that strategy, all that we will succeed in doing is to strengthen the very thing we wish to defeat, our toxic patterns.

Our young man from the last chapter, for example, may do well for a time, thinking he has finally walked away from his childhood and defeated his past. Then one day, he may fall hopelessly in love with a beautiful young woman, who, in due course, will come to treat him as contemptuously and critically as his mother ever had. Or, he may land his dream job only to discover that his boss is as verbally abusive to him as his father once had been. Or even worse, he may simultaneously fall in love with the wrong woman and get a new job with a boss who is highly toxic to him.

The lesson is clear. What we repress and deny is highly charged, although we may not feel it, and it is always dangerous to our interests, although we may not know it.

I once wrote a short verse to describe the potency of unconscious toxicity. That toxicity has a purpose and a mission of its own, which is always antagonistic to our conscious hopes and plans. Its purpose is to defeat us by defeating our dreams and to render us frustrated and unfulfilled by continually repeating the toxic patterns of our past.

> *Within each and everyone of us,*
> *Lives a shadow that never sleeps.*
> *Its goal is deprivation.*
> *It exults in our defeat.*

External accomplishment does not automatically translate into inner achievement. Material success cannot compensate for internal emptiness and the loss of the Self. Greed is not a substitute for inner peace, and desire can never tell us who we are.

Greed

Those among us whose only goal is the acquisition of power and wealth rarely see beyond their greed to what it is they truly need. When people are in greed mode, they become so enmeshed in craving what they want, and so absorbed by the fear that they might not get it, that they become totally oblivious to the silent voice of their deepest longing. Their attachment to their greed makes their alienation difficult to resolve.

Whenever greed and desire are the paramount values in the psyche, the soul is undervalued, its importance denied, and its power misunderstood. The person in greed mode lives on the surface of his being. The hidden resources of his deeper nature lie untapped, unable to feed his surface strength. He is split off from his true self and his deeper life purpose. While he may not know it, he is working against his true self and his future. His collapse is inevitable.

One day, the comfort of external success will give way to the dejection of internal defeat, and like Septimius before him, he will be haunted by the long shadow enveloping his life, knowing that he has failed at his most important task. For those in greed mode, the more success their endeavors bring them, the more their greed seems to consume them. That greed will take them on an unexpected journey as they travel farther into emptiness and further from themselves. Success is not always the antidote to greed. In fact, it often adds fuel to its fire.

The Glamour of Success

It is highly ironic to be sure, but getting what we desire often leads to disappointment. The initial sense of excitement that accompanies the march of desire toward its objective soon gives way to the inevitable experience of boredom and emptiness once that objective has been attained. Despite getting what we wanted, nothing within has really changed. Fear, greed, and desire are still with us, while our soul and spirit remain outside our conscious experience. As a result of our alienation from the deeper aspects of ourselves, the magic of getting what we want fails to endure beyond the initial sense of excitement it brings us. We went up for awhile and briefly forgot ourselves. Then we came back down and had to face our reality again.

Getting what we wanted did not relieve the weight of our lives or reduce the burden of our living. It did not bring us lasting peace, fill us with a brighter light, or make us more joyful. It failed to make us more conscious, end our silent suffering, or liberate us from our darkness. While success can last for a long time, it will fail to satisfy us for more than a short time. That is the curse of success. Happiness is always over the next hill.

Without recourse to our soul and spirit, we have no way to find our center or to be at peace. Instead, we are assigned by our failure in integrating the two major aspects of our system to live between conflicting waves of emotion. The promise of desire leads to disappointment. The hunger of greed leads to unhappiness. Both greed and desire lead us farther away from our real self. This is the seduction of greed and desire. Greed and desire can never complete us or make us whole. Instead, they create more distance between how we are manifesting ourselves in the world and who we really are.

Incomplete Emotion and Internal Distance

Greed and desire are born from our loss of connection to our soul and the void that loss creates within our psyche. When we lose our connection to our soul, we lose our ability to be a source of unconditional love. When we lose the ability to be a channel of unconditional love, we no longer know who we are. Greed and desire then become our response to the pain of losing our higher connection.

If we don't find the one clear voice of our true self, we will find ourselves swamped by the many disingenuous voices of our false selves. All these voices clamor for our attention, each one greedily demanding that we give it what it wants. Each voice claims to be our one true voice and tells us that if we get it what it wants, it will provide the answer to our unhappiness. However, the manifestation of each desire soon becomes another false hope. Since we don't know how to reclaim our ability to love unconditionally, we cling instead to greed and desire. We will cling to greed and desire until we integrate the physical and supra-physical aspects of our system.

Toxicity and Desire

The strength of our desire nature is determined by the degree of toxic emotion in our system. Toxic emotions create internal distance from our real self. Once that internal distance exists, most of us will attempt to close it by using desire rather than unconditional love in seeking fulfillment. Of course this strategy creates the opposite result of what we intended. Instead of leading to fulfillment, desire creates more internal distance between who we really are and what we have become.

Desire does not shorten our way home, but will, instead, add many unnecessary detours to our journey. While the pursuit of what we desire will not cure our emptiness, it does add to our desperation.

The Thrust of Desire

The internal distance from our real self that desire creates is the terrain of the negative ego. It is a terrain that we protect by our denial of its existence. One reason we resist facing ourselves is that the natural thrust of desire is outward. Desire seduces us with the idea that the answer to being lost, empty, confused, or unhappy can be found in the material world, rather than within ourselves. What we find in the material world, however, are material things. Material things can prop us up or puff us up, but they will never reveal who we really are. By leading us outward in the search for our truth, desire leads us in the wrong direction. In pursuing the material world to the detriment of our inner world, desire leads us away from confronting our shadow, which is comprised of our unresolved toxic energies.

The paradox of desire is that while it encourages us to walk away from our darkness, it is only by walking toward our darkness that we will go free. Inner darkness is always the antagonist of inner freedom. In many ways, desire is the agent of that darkness. As long as desire rules the psyche, that darkness will remain intact, and the internal distance we must travel to find ourselves is in constant danger of growing longer.

The Negative Ego's Strategy

The negative ego's strategy is to keep us occupied in vain pursuits that feed it but do not feed us. If it can keep us focused on our greed and desire, the negative ego is assured of maintaining its power. To defeat the negative ego at its game, we must realize that we are not our shame. The territory of toxic emotion that the negative ego tries to hide from the world is not who we are. It is what prevents us from being who we are. To identify ourselves with our shame is to keep ourselves from our freedom. It is the error of identification that the negative ego wants us to make. It is the mistake that drives us to utilize our desire nature to flee from facing whatever false self we have erected and have come to believe that we are. The whole rationale behind the power of desire is that if we succeed in fleeing from the pain of our shame, we can hide ourselves in material pleasure. The problem with that rationale is that pleasure always ends. Sooner or later, our pain will return and overwhelm us. As long as shame exists, it can never be entirely silenced.

What we must eventually realize is that what we fail to confront is much more dangerous to us than that what we choose to face. What we shrink from facing shrinks us. While we can actualize our desires, our desires cannot actualize us. Our soul contains our identity, our path, and our purpose. Our desire nature is the adversary of our higher connection.

When we finally realize that the three forces of alienation, fear, greed, and desire, are a dead end and lead nowhere, we are finally ready to enter the Elimination Zone and begin the path of personal evolution. What we need to keep in mind as we enter the Elimination Zone is that when we stand up to our fear, our fear will stand down. We regain our power when we confront the inner darkness that would otherwise diminish us.

Conquering Desire

Sri Aurobindo's spiritual partner, The Mother, once wrote that, "To conquer a desire brings more joy than to satisfy it."* When we conquer a desire, we take back the specific part of our power that we had invested in our desire nature. Every time we conquer a desire we strengthen our real self and weaken the lock that the negative ego and desire nature have over us. Every time we overcome a desire, we shorten the internal distance we must travel to reach our soul and claim our inner light. Every piece of power that we reclaim from our desire nature lessens the gap between who we think we are and who we really are.

Desire will never complete us because it leaves our inner darkness and negative ego intact. The more we chase our desires, the more we feed our restlessness. As our restlessness grows, our desires intensify. As one desire after another fails to elevate our lives in any lasting way, we replace those desires with others. The failure of desire leads to the birth of more desires. The more desire fails us, the more dominant our desire nature becomes.

The only solution to the problem of desire is to find our wholeness through integrating the physical and supra-physical aspects of our system. When we clear our toxicity we are well on the way to finding our wholeness.

Different Poles of Experience

If we do not clear our toxicity, our soul cannot take its rightful position of influence within our psyche, and our evolution will be unconscious and minimal at best. It is difficult to grow when we are not consciously involved with our consciousness. Growth that is forced to proceed along strictly unconscious lines is growth that advances at a glacial pace.

We ignite our growth when we choose to participate in it. The difference between unconscious and conscious growth is the difference between riding on a donkey and flying in a jet. There is no real comparison.

Consciousness and desire then, are different poles of experience. Consciousness is the positive pole. It quickens the pace of our struggle

---

* Aurobindo, A Practical Guide to Integral Yoga, p.122

for more internal light and a deeper connection with our soul. It forces us to face the unhealed parts of our nature and then liberates us from our toxicity so we may find ourselves.

 Desire is the negative pole of experience. It keeps us churning in the machinations of the negative ego. As long as we are stirred up and involved in one drama after another, we will not find peace, establish a connection to our soul, or go forward in our growth. Drama keeps us involved and preoccupied with the objects of our desire so that we are unaware of our emptiness and our loss of our real self.

The covert purpose of the negative ego is to keep the soul from entering the psyche. If it succeeds in that purpose, it will remain in control of the psyche and will not have to endure its own transformation into a healthy ego.

Desire and the negative ego are the great antagonists to wholeness and completion. That is their role in the great play of human evolution. They are not our friends. To defeat them, we must develop our inner light, integrate the two sides of our system, and reclaim our ability to love unconditionally. When we have integrated ourselves, we will be able to turn away from the path of most resistance with little further resistance.

The Negative Ego's Dilemma

Meanwhile, the negative ego has a dilemma on its hands. While it feels safe in moving outward in the world, as opposed to moving inward to face the toxicity buried in its host's system, it will never find lasting safety in doing so. The primary role of the negative ego is to protect its host from having to feel his original pain and fear again. It does this by burying those toxic experiences in his body, determined to keep them out of sight at all costs. If the host never has to feel them again, he can pretend they no longer exist. Unfortunately, denial is not a solution. It simply creates more internal distance between the host's conscious mind and his subconscious afflictions. That distance doesn't strengthen him. Instead, it undermines him by empowering his unconscious toxicity.

As we know, we cannot heal the splits in our nature until we raise the pain hidden in our body to the surface of our conscious mind. Given that operational truth, the negative ego cannot succeed in *its* primary mission of protecting us from pain. However, it does a very good job in distracting us from *our* primary mission in life, which is to realize who we really are. The truth is that the ego cannot protect us from fear and pain. The fact that pain is buried in our body means that we will attract more of it into our life, no matter how strong our resistance to it is or how powerful our sense of denial about it may be. As long as unresolved issues plague the subconscious, the will of the subconscious is negatively polarized. When an aspect of the will is negatively polarized, it holds the entire will hostage.

The negative ego then has little real security beyond how well it can keep us in the dark about our own darkness. A key goal of the relationship between the negative ego and the three forces of alienation is to keep us trapped in a limited experience of reality, where the most important parts of our nature are never seen or experienced.

Service

The truth the negative ego cannot grasp is that we always feel more fulfilled when we serve the well-being of others than when we adhere strictly to our own self-interest. Giving of ourselves enriches us more than taking from others ever could.

The richest among us are those who have succeeded in their inner journey. Their consciousness is filled with inner light. They have integrated their system and are whole. Their spirit, soul, mind, personality, emotions, and physical body are in alignment. Because of that alignment, their outer activities are in harmony with their essential nature. What they choose to do reflects who they really are. They have no internal resistance and no toxic shadow to deprive them of fulfillment. Instead, they have the support of a higher power in their endeavors. The "force" is with them. The world benefits from their vision, their work, their love, and their words. They are not here to take. They are here to serve and to give.

The purpose of the path of personal evolution is to help us find ourselves and succeed in our life's journey. Life works when we are whole. It is a much more difficult proposition when we have not integrated the physical and supra-physical aspects of our nature. The world needs us all to be successful in that endeavor.

six CLEARING THE DARKNESS

*What strange beings we are! That sitting in hell at the
bottom of the dark, we're afraid of our own immortality.*

Rumi

*A human being is part of the whole called by us the
universe... We experience ourselves, our thoughts and
feelings as something separate from the rest. A kind
of optical delusion of consciousness. This delusion is
a kind of prison for us, restricting us to our personal
desires and affection for a few persons nearest to us.
Our task must be to free ourselves from the prison
by widening our circle of compassion to embrace all
living creatures... We shall require a substantially new
manner of thinking if mankind is to survive.*

Albert Einstein

The Three Primary Tasks of the Elimination Zone

The Elimination Zone has three primary tasks that must be completed
before we can move on to the Integration Zone and the next phase of
conscious evolution. These three primary tasks are to:

- *Clear unconscious toxicity from the psyche.*

- *Deflate the negative ego and defuse the desire nature.*

- *Create an opening through which the soul may enter the psyche.*

Elimination and Revolution

The main purpose of the Elimination Zone is to shift the balance of power in the psyche from the negative ego to the soul. Since the source of the negative ego's power is seated in the repressed emotional toxicity hidden in the psyche, the transfer of power from the negative ego to the soul is always preceded by emotional upheaval. The purpose of that upheaval is to clear unconscious toxicity from the psyche. This catharsis is a revolution, a change that initiates a new order of authority in the psyche and marks the beginning of the path of personal evolution. When that purge takes place, the negative ego loses its power base. The negative ego is no longer in control, and the psyche is no longer split and divided.

As a consequence of that revolution, things in our life that no longer work will depart of their own volition or be shown the door. Outmoded working and living conditions, relationships, beliefs, and lifestyles will fall away. Conditions and opportunities that are more in harmony with our true nature will begin to take their place.

A Shift in Consciousness

One of the governing principles of all true internal work is that a shift in consciousness leads to a change in circumstances. As we move forward in the work of personal evolution, there will be several such shifts. Each shift will upgrade and elevate our life experience. Personal evolution has the potential to compress the work of several lifetimes into a few lifetimes, or even one. How long the work will take depends upon our level of evolution and our readiness for the journey. Regardless of where we may think we are or how advanced we think we might be, the journey begins in the same way for all of us. Entering the Elimination Zone and purging our unconscious toxicity is the foundation for all further advances in consciousness.

By far, the most important of the three goals in the Elimination Zone is the first one. When we clear unconscious toxicity from our system we open the way for the other goals of the elimination phase to unfold in rapid succession. Clearing unconscious toxicity is the necessary foundation for everything that will follow. If we disregard this reality and try to overcome the negative ego or create access for the soul without first clearing our toxicity, we will find the challenge insurmountable. Clearing unconscious toxicity is fundamental to the growth process and must be done diligently and deeply.

Even after we move beyond the Elimination Zone and enter the next two growth zones, more toxic material may surface unexpectedly. The reason more toxicity may surface in the next stages of our development is that as we move forward with our internal growth, more spiritual light will flow through our system. As that light flows through us it will force whatever darkness we haven't found to the surface to be cleared. If we fail to clear our toxicity, we will fail to find our wholeness, fail to realize who we are, and fall short in fulfilling our higher purpose.

Approaching the Unconscious

Opening the door to our unconscious toxicity may in the beginning prove to be a bit more difficult than we might imagine. After all, we are dealing with the realm of the irrational, the obscure, and the hidden. It is not a realm that most of us are used to dealing with. Its currents are unpredictable and uncertain. The subconscious as a rule does not yield its secrets easily or surrender them on demand. Rather, it laughs at and mocks the conscious affirmations we make asserting we have overcome our subconscious resistance and disarmed our fear, shame, and guilt. The subconscious knows that the toxicity buried in its vaults cannot be disarmed or controlled by the assertions of our conscious mind. We can't wish ourselves out of the clutches of our toxicity, but with diligent effort we can bring our toxicity to the gates of the conscious mind. The arrival of unconscious toxicity at the doors of the conscious mind is the moment of transformation. While that moment may elicit our deepest fears, facing those fears leads to the integration of the physical and supra-physical aspects of our system.

Our initial attempts to enter the shadow world of the subconscious often reveal a formidable opponent who is skilled at hiding and excels in resisting detection. A few screams, kicks, and knocks in the hopes of unleashing a torrent of buried emotion are not always going to be enough to open the barriers separating the conscious mind from the subconscious. Persistence and determination are important qualities to bring to the fight for clarity.

Do not forget that the negative ego's intention is to hide our pain from us. It invariably exceeds its mandate by hiding itself in our repressed toxicity as well. The secret to the negative ego's longevity is our fear of facing what we fear most. Our resistance to facing those fears keeps fear alive, increases the negative ego's authority in our lives, and prevents us from integrating our system. Whenever fear is present and remains unchallenged, the negative ego avoids exposure and maintains its dominion.

The Path Begins in Darkness

There is no obvious, straight, or clear road through the dim maze of the subconscious. We fight our way into the light by challenging the dark and hidden forces inside us. When we finally challenge our inner darkness, we begin to forge our real path. That path does not begin until we face our darkness.

We start where we feel anxiety, fear, discomfort, grief, sadness, rage, or pain. We start with our most prominent, obvious, and available negative emotions. Those emotions are the triggers that will help us unlock the door sealing our toxicity from our conscious mind. If we continue to feel and express those emotions until they become mobile and rise to meet our conscious mind, we will defeat the hidden toxic events they conceal.

We mobilize our toxicity by feeling our negative emotions as intensely as we can, then giving them a sound that expresses those feelings. That sound may be a guttural Urhhh!, or an Oohh!, or a string of curses. It really doesn't matter what the sound is as long as it conveys our repressed feelings. By consciously expressing those feelings, we will eventually reach the stream of unconscious toxicity that lies behind them. When that toxic stream surfaces, we will no longer have to consciously force the process because those unconscious emotions will surge through us, and we will feel and express them with unexpected intensity. When that happens, the toxic events associated with the expression of those emotions will be released from our system.

❦ The Secret of Personal Evolution

The path that starts in the light, stays in the light, and ends in the light, never finds the bright light of the soul. We don't evolve by avoiding our darkness. We evolve by facing our darkness, and face it we must. We can't go up and elevate our life if we are unwilling to go down and eliminate our toxicity. When we clear our darkness we create more room for the light of our soul to shine brightly in our lives. Unconscious toxicity is the fuel of conscious growth.

If we try to "stay" in the light and avoid facing the darkness of our unconscious toxicity, we will not grow further. Our light will not burn brighter, and we will be unable to build the bridge to our soul. We might gain a method to reduce daily stress but not a means to elevate our life. Without clearing our toxic content, we cannot open ourselves to our soul or integrate the higher facets of our nature into our life in any cohesive way. Conquering our inner darkness is the secret to finding our path, our identity, and our purpose.

The Playground Bully

Since the negative ego is rooted in unconscious toxicity and draws its strength from our repressed shame, clearing the toxic shame from our system will deprive the ego of its heavyweight status in the psyche. It will no longer be the playground bully, using fear to bind us in the darkness and suppress the superior voice of the soul. Of course, the negative ego does not fall easily, nor does it fall all at once. That would be far too easy. Usually, we must process several layers of unconscious toxicity before the negative ego begins to lose its strength. Nevertheless, every layer and toxic experience we clear diminishes the power the negative ego has over us until that power is fully deflated.

Defeating the negative ego is a goal that often evades the grasp of dedicated people, who have pursued their growth and spiritual development for years. Much of that failure is not due to lack of effort, level of commitment, or degree of consistent application, but rather to the use of inadequate methods that do not go deep enough, reach far enough, or have enough power to provide the desired results.

Clearing the Darkness

To go deep into the dark labyrinth of the psyche requires a bright inner light and the application of a pure spiritual power. If you find someone who has the light and the power, is highly experienced, and has a proven track record, my suggestion is that you work with that person until you have cleared your toxicity. Don't let go of them until that work is done. A really fine healer or therapist is a very rare commodity.

The goal of personal evolution is to become strong, independent, centered in the soul, and self-sufficient. However, when you are engaged in the deep clearing work that elimination requires, it is wiser and safer to work with someone who has the necessary experience to take you through the Elimination Zone, rather than to attempt that journey yourself. You have a much better chance of clearing your unconscious toxicity if you work with a skilled healer than if you throw caution to the wind and attempt to do it on your own.

Seeking Help

There are two reasons for seeking help to go through the Elimination Zone. The first is that few people have the requisite inner power and light to do the work on their own. Secondly, fewer still have the wisdom and experience to navigate the unknown shoals of their subconscious minds. When it comes to swimming in the uncharted waters of the subconscious, it is best to have an objective and experienced professional to guide you. This is one area where the wise person will both invest the time and bear the financial cost in order to get clear.

If you are determined to navigate the Elimination Zone on your own, here are some suggestions to help guide you in your efforts. The following method comes from my personal journey through the darkest regions of my own subconscious. I was able to discharge my toxicity successfully because of the confluence of four factors. First, I had years of experience in helping clients go through the Elimination Zone and clear their unconscious toxicity. I knew the territory of the subconscious well and had a well-defined concept of what might happen when I entered it. Second, because of all the energy work I had already done with my clients, my inner light and power was sufficient to the task. Third, my conscious intent to clear my remaining toxicity was very high. I knew what was at stake, and I was determined not to fail. Fourth, I was and am emotionally stable and able to handle whatever might arise from the depths of my subconscious. If you're not sure of your own stability and inner strength, do not attempt this work on your own.

Even with all of these advantages, the task of encountering the deepest elements of my shadow and clearing them from my system was anything but easy. It was a long and arduous journey that took me far longer to complete than I had originally thought it would. If you wish to attempt this work on your own, proceed slowly and cautiously. If you run into a problem, don't be afraid to seek professional help.

The Method for Clearing the Hidden Past

My formula for mobilizing my own toxicity was simple and straightforward. Every day, I would lie on my healing table and feel where the discomfort and the negative feelings were most obvious in my body at that particular time. After I had located those places of discomfort in my body, I would imagine myself entering an elevator in my mind. After entering the elevator, I would see myself taking it down my spinal column until it reached the place in my body where I felt the most discomfort. When I reached that location, I would step out of the elevator and step into my feelings. As I merged with my discomfort, I would intensify whatever I was feeling by imagining that I was turning up the number on a dial from one to seven. With every turn of the dial, I would let those feelings become stronger until they reached their point of maximum impact at number seven on the dial. As my negative feelings became stronger and more focused, I would make guttural sounds as if they were coming out of the place in my body where those feelings were stored. I would make those sounds over and over again until I felt that I had done all that I could do in that particular session. After several weeks of working in this manner, my toxicity softened up and became more mobile.

Mobility is the key to transformation. When my toxicity became mobile, it poured out of me, day after day after day, until it was completely discharged. During that period, I cried a lot. Sometimes I'd scream and rage. Sometimes I'd wail. Sometimes I'd shake and vibrate. Sometimes I'd get ice cold. Sometimes I'd burn up. Sometimes it all happened at once. Eventually it ended. My dark night of the soul was over, and I stood free and clear with an open door in my system for the light of the spirit to flow through to the core of my being.

In my case, the toxic material that emerged and needed to be processed came mainly from past lifetimes. My soul brought that material to the surface because I had processed much of my material from this lifetime in earlier work with my mentor and teacher. Those past lifetimes were next in the queue that my soul had set up for processing toxic material.

Most people find that when they begin this work, the material most likely to emerge first is their toxicity from this lifetime. Other people will find that the material that surfaces first is from a past lifetime. The reason for the seeming discrepancy in which material emerges first is that your soul will push those incidents to the surface that are ready to be processed so that you might go forward with your life. Sometimes, that material is from this lifetime, and sometimes it is from a previous lifetime.

Clearing the Present

While clearing the unconscious emotional toxicity from your past may be too complex a task to take on by yourself, clearing your current stress and negativity is a task that you can work through on your own. Let's say, for example, that you've had a stressful day filled with conflict and hostility. You leave work feeling tense, angry, and worried. Your first thought when you walk through your front door and greet your family is to get a drink or two to soothe your nerves. You want to forget what happened as quickly as you can, and ignore those troublesome feelings that have tied your stomach up in knots. Your anger, however, is not eager to cooperate with your intentions and will not readily accede to your wishes. Anger is an agitated, aggressive, restless, and unhappy energy in need of an outlet and in search of a target. It cannot be stilled or pacified for long. Unless you transform your anger it will manifest in unexpected ways that are destructive to both yourself and other people.

You've finished one drink now and are finally beginning to unwind. Your stomach is loosening up. You are finally able to breathe again. Then your spouse or one of your children barges into your study and asks you an innocent question. Before you can catch yourself you are taking the weight of your frustration out on them. "Leave me alone! I've had a bad day," you scream. "Can't you see that I need to be by myself for a few minutes? Is that too damn much to ask? Go away!" It's not the way you intended to react, but you couldn't help yourself. The words just slipped out of your mouth before you could stop yourself from saying them. Once they are out there you can't take them back. The anger that hurt you in the workplace is now hurting those you love at home. A single, momentary slip of the tongue is all it took to cause emotional damage. Dinner is not pleasant, the air charged with unexpressed emotion. No one says much. Instead, everyone retreats into his or her own world, upset, angry, and silent.

While that is painful enough, the events of the evening do not end at the dinner table. Every family member carries that toxicity with them into the next day. The toxicity in their systems will, in turn, infect many of the people they interact with perpetuating the toxicity and expanding its reach.

As the above example illustrates, your failure to process negative emotions can have serious consequences beyond your own experience. Instead of trying to assuage your anger and hope it goes away on its own a far better approach to dealing with toxic emotion involves confronting and clearing your negativity as it arises. When you confront your negativity as it occurs you regain your balance and gain more power, clarity, and confidence. When you clear your negativity you will be less prone to creating more negative karma. The opposite, however, is also true. When you ignore your anger, hoping that it will go away of its own accord, you lose your power and balance. By ignoring your anger you put yourself in harm's way, for you never know when or how that anger might surface and cause you to explode. When your anger does surface the one thing you can count on is that the way you express it will not be in your best interests. Angry people are never at peace. They are karma generating machines.

The Clearing Technique

The good news is that you can use the same technique to clear current negativity that I described in detail earlier in the chapter to clear toxicity from the more distant past.

1. First, lie down somewhere in your house where you feel safe and comfortable and won't be bothered.

2. Take a few deep breaths and relax. Shake your legs and arms to release your surface tension. Now play your day back in your mind, making sure to reconnect with your feelings as you review the events that caused you to have those negative emotions.

3. After you have reviewed your day and recalled your emotions, visualize an elevator in your mind and imagine taking it down your spine to the place in your body where you feel the most discomfort. When you arrive at that place in your body step out of the elevator and step into your discomfort.

4. Embrace the negative feelings stored in your body. Feel them fully. Concentrate on your anger, frustration, and shame. Now imagine that there is a dial that can turn up the intensity of your feelings as you turn the number on the dial from one up to seven. With every

turn of the dial your feelings become stronger. As you reach seven on the dial your feelings become very intense.

5. As your feelings reach the point of maximum intensity express them verbally. Make guttural, primitive, non-verbal sounds, scream, curse if you need to, cry, kick the carpet, punch the air. Just go with whatever your body wants to do. Don't censor or judge yourself. If you feel self-conscious and ridiculous as you do this, so what. No one is watching. Remember that you are by yourself in a safe environment. Feeling foolish is a small price to pay for feeling better. So go ahead, give yourself permission to feel and look foolish. Be vocal, shake your limbs, and get all that negative emotion out of your system. Just remember to stay safe and not proceed so vigorously that you might hurt yourself. When you are engaged in clearing negative emotion it is always best to be laying down on a thick carpet on the floor, or on your bed. If neither of those options is available to you a good sofa or a comfortable easy chair will do.

6. When you have completed clearing your negativity rest for a moment. Then re-enter the elevator and travel in it up your spinal column to your head. When the elevator returns to your head step out of the elevator and return to normal consciousness. Relax for a few minutes and allow your system to integrate and balance itself.

When you do this process on a daily basis you will find that it becomes simple and routine to clear your system of current negativity. One of the great benefits of clearing the present in this manner is that it will make it easier for you to clear the deeper past. Not only is the technique the same, but as you clear your current stress you are also softening up and mobilizing the deeper toxicity in your system without realizing it. Mobilizing the buried toxicity of the past makes that toxicity much easier to clear when you are ready to take it on. So, rather than starting with what is difficult, the distant past, start with what is easy, the present situation.

While clearing the present is essential to your health and well-being, clearing the hidden past is essential to evolving beyond where you are. Both tasks are critical to integrating your system and accelerating your life momentum.

The Lethal Nature of Unconscious Toxicity

If we permit unconscious toxicity to remain entrenched in our system, however, it will recreate the dysfunctional patterns of our original wounding experience. The wounds of the past will become the wounds of the present. The way we once bled will be the way we bleed again. Subconscious determinism will override the will of the conscious mind, severely limiting our ability to experience real inner freedom or find fulfillment.

When the subconscious contains hidden toxicity the people and situations we draw to us may seem to be very different from those that were toxic to us in the past, but the underlying patterns we experience in our encounters with them will be the same. They will still carry the same toxic charge for us as the people who originally shamed us, and they will infect us with that same toxicity all over again.

I once had a client, a female attorney, who was divorcing her husband, who happened to be a judge. She constantly complained that her husband was dry, distant, cold, and critical. While he may have had the perfect personality for a judge, he had the wrong one for a marriage. He constantly put her down and made her feel inadequate. Her self-esteem was virtually non-existent. When she first came to see me, her system was full of rage toward all men.

In our first few sessions, we were able to clear some of her rage. That clearing created enough reflective space in her system for me to ask her about her childhood and her parents. When I asked her about her father, she answered that he had been warm, outgoing, engaging, and funny, nothing at all like her husband.

"Was your childhood a happy one?" I asked.

"Not really," she admitted in a low voice.

"Why?" I asked.

"Well," she started hesitantly, "My father was warm and funny, but he picked on me and made fun of me! He made me feel really inadequate and ashamed of myself, although I'm sure he didn't mean to."

With that confession, she burst into tears. I let her cry, making no attempt to console her. Consolation, like sympathy, validates the inner victim and interferes with the clearing process. Consoling her would have kept her rage intact, stopped her progress, and deprived her of the opportunity to discharge an important piece of her childhood shame. When she finished crying and became more peaceful, I pointed out the connection between her father and her husband.

"So," I began, "while your husband and father are nothing alike, at least in terms of their personality, they are very much alike with regard to the quality that wounded and shamed you. Both of them were critical of you. Both of them made fun of you. Both of them put you down. Both of them made you feel inadequate and worthless. Your father caused your original shame. Your husband reopened that wound. Chronologically, the wounding events of your childhood are many years behind you, but the toxic emotion from those experiences is still very present in your system. Those emotions haven't been banished. Instead, they have traveled with you into the present. Although hidden, they control your life.

"Shame is a very powerful ongoing emotional event. It is not over just because the time it happened in is past. Time doesn't separate you from your toxic emotions, as it separates you from the historical events of the past. If your toxicity remains unconscious, it will continue to terrorize you until you clear your childhood shame. If you don't clear your shame, you will pull someone else into your life that will do the same thing to you. If your childhood dynamics had been more positive, you never would have married your husband in the first place. The source of your problem lies in your relationship to your father. Your husband is the result of that originating pattern."

"Great!" she said, feeling frustrated by the task ahead of her. She had come to me to get over her husband. Now she had to deal with something even more difficult and overwhelming, her father.

"It only seems impossible now," I told her. "The reality is that it should be fairly simple to clear the childhood shame from your system. The worst is over. You have faced the truth. When you know the truth you know what to do. The truth about your toxicity is a map that reveals your path to wholeness. Right now, your path goes through your relationship to your father. Every time you reveal and redeem another layer of your toxicity, you will discover more of your path and stand in more of your light. We make our way to our truth, step by step. Every step we take brings us more freedom. Much of life is about overcoming the negative. Since we all have had a different life experience, we each have a unique path to discover who we really are. This is your path."

"Is this about the worst thing you've ever had to deal with?" she asked in the wounded voice of a child.

"No," I replied. "It's actually one of the easier dilemmas I have faced. This should be routine. The good news is that we now know where we're going. The next step of your path is clearly defined. Your material is fairly mobile and should be easy to move. We should get through it quickly."

"Thank God!"

Original Sin, Originating Shame

As this case indicates, while the participants in our toxic drama often change, the central theme of that drama does not. This is the psychological equivalent of original sin. An originating trauma becomes an ongoing problem. We rarely want to face our shame because shame, at its core and in its darkest places, makes us feel fatally flawed, unfixable, and unworthy. To feel unfixable is unendurable.

The most common solution to the problem of shame is to deny that it exists and then flee desperately into our desire nature as fast as we can. Unfortunately, our desires are not well equipped to save us. Instead of releasing us from the oppressive weight of our toxicity and the toxic situations we draw to us, they divert us from the hidden issues that dominate our lives. While desire may distract us, it can never redeem us.

In my client's case, the future repetition of the original problem arrived in a compelling disguise, packaged in a different personality and starring in a different role. If we allow ourselves to be distracted by the superficial differences provided by an appealing disguise, we will fall victim to the devious power that our denied shame possesses to reach into the future and sabotage our life.

Immortalizing Shame

The truth emerges when the surface differences have been shorn of their camouflage and the heart of the matter is all that remains. We cannot evade our shame. If we try to evade it, we will only succeed in empowering it in two important ways. First, a toxic event that remains unconscious *retains* its power. Second, when we allow our shame to retain its power, we make it *immortal*. The consequences of immortalizing our shame are immense. As long as we permit shame to function with impunity in our psyches, we will never be whole; we will never be happy; we will never be fulfilled; we will not go forward; we will not evolve; we will never know who we really are, or what our true purpose is. Toxic shame defeats the true purpose of our lives.

Chronic psychic bleeding, like that experienced by my client, carries serious and immediate consequences. It steals our energy, deprives us of clarity, and upsets our emotional balance. In the end it leaves us powerless, victimized, enraged, and confused. As long as unconscious toxicity sits in our system, the door to the soul is closed to further contact, no matter how much we might meditate or pray, or how many hours of Yoga we might do a day.

Nor does physical death end the tyranny of shame. Everything we failed to resolve while on earth must be resolved upon our return to earth. When we die, the emotional energy associated with our experience of shame leaves with us, becoming a part of our soul complex and a component of our unresolved history as an incarnated entity. Since shame survives death, it becomes more deeply embedded in the subconscious in our next incarnation and more unavailable to us. When we don't deal with our shame, we immortalize it. What we postpone ends up owning us. When we immortalize our shame, we increase its potency.

Shame: Past and Present

When we have failed to face our shame, the unresolved shame of the past becomes the unknown shame the present. When the source of our shame is unknown, it is much more difficult to connect the patterns of the past to the events of the present. Unresolved shame becomes unconscious shame. We don't know and can't remember why we feel the way we do. As shame becomes unconscious, the odds increase substantially that it will remain immortal. One of the more disturbing consequences of immortalizing shame is that it greatly increases the internal distance that must be traversed if we are to become the person we were always meant to be.

Real Self vs. Shamed Self

Our real self is not a part of material creation. The real self, unlike the physical body that houses it for a specific incarnation, does not originate in the material world. It belongs to the higher realms of the spirit and is unconditionally immortal. Nothing can change its true nature or destroy it.

Shame, in contrast, is a part of material creation. Its immortality is conditional. It only becomes immortal if we refuse to face and clear it. When we finally confront it, it loses its immortal status and is destroyed. It will plague us no more.

Everything in life has a price. Nothing comes without a cost. The price of freedom and fulfillment is overcoming everything within you that is not the real you. The cost of healing your shame is finding it, facing it, feeling it, and clearing it.

SUMMARY OF MAJOR POINTS

- *Unconscious toxicity ties us to the past.* While unconscious toxicity remains in the psyche, the past is prologue to the future.

- *We strengthen our shame when we refuse to face it.* What we don't clear becomes repetitive and immortal.

❧ *Unconscious toxicity is both kingmaker and spoiler.* It gives the ego its crowning power, while preventing the soul from claiming its rightful place of authority.

❧ *Unconscious toxicity splits us off from our spiritual nature, our happiness and our fulfillment.* When toxic elements hide within our psyche, we cannot be whole or advance our evolution beyond where we are now. As long as the negative ego holds the reigns of power, we will never realize our true identity or find our higher purpose.

❧ *As long as unconscious toxicity remains in the psyche, the negative ego will retain its hegemony over the soul, and inner balance will be impossible to achieve.* When we regain our inner balance, we reopen the doors of possibility. The future will not be a restatement of past toxicity, but an opportunity to increase our inner light.

❧ *Inner balance emerges when two conditions are fulfilled.* First, we burn up our shame. Second, our soul emerges as the rightful ruler of the psyche. When we regain our balance with the soul becoming the main authority in the psyche, we have the opportunity to discover who we really are and what our higher purpose is.

❧ *When we burn up our unconscious toxicity we jump-start our growth.* With the removal of the hidden blocks in our system our life momentum turns positive and progress toward the goal of Self-realization accelerates dramatically.

The Doctrine of False Piety

While it may not be apparent to everyone, the real business of life is "growing" our consciousness. In the old archetype of spirituality, the pursuit of consciousness was accompanied by self-sacrifice. Consciousness was associated with martyrdom and a substantial increase in suffering. The physical world was thought of as the devil's playground, and the acquisition of material goods was strongly discouraged. To do otherwise was to be corrupted and to fail. Self-denial was seen as the essence of piety.

Enforced denial, however, creates a powerful attraction for what has been denied. Deny someone something he really wants, and you create a craving in that person for what has been denied him. Deny someone something necessary to his life, and you will only succeed in tying that person tighter to the object of that denial, while at the same time creating in him a great deal of fear and guilt about the issue in general. The end result of enforced denial is that what has been disallowed will become a more powerful theme within that person's psyche than the search for consciousness ever could. What one can't have will dominate one's life. In the end, enforced denial only strengthens the desire nature. It is counterproductive to one's growth and evolution.

Enforced denial then, often leads to the opposite of its intended result. Instead of smoothing and quickening the path to truth, it creates more internal obstacles to be unraveled. It dams up and subverts psychic energy. If you don't think this is true, consider the plight of the Catholic Church with its central doctrine of celibacy for all priests. Would the tragedy of pedophilia in the priesthood have happened if the doctrine of celibacy no longer existed and priests were free to marry? You don't find much mention of children being sexually abused by ministers, rabbis, and imams, where the clergy in these respective religions are free to marry and raise a family.

Consciousness and Congruency

In the new archetype of consciousness, the world and the pursuit of spiritual growth are no longer in conflict but have become congruent. The world is not the enemy, but rather the reflection of our consciousness. We no longer have to be rigid, self-sacrificing, and self-righteous in the attempt to be clear and whole. In fact, those attributes will not only prevent us from being whole, but are also clear signs that we have failed in our attempt to do so.

It is certainly acceptable to do good works in the world and have material abundance. Moreover, when we are whole and have what we need, we are less consumed by material possessions than we are when we lack them.

It is only common sense to realize that if others benefit from our good works, so should we. Giving and receiving are equal parts of a larger whole. When we can receive the love of others, as well as give our love to them, we keep the positive energy flowing forward in our life.

We gain positive life momentum when we clear the toxicity from our system. We strengthen and expand that momentum when we give of ourselves and allow others to give back to us. Wholeness is a circle, made up of equal parts of giving and receiving. When we operate within the dynamics of that circle we will experience abundance and joy.

seven THE GAME OF LIFE

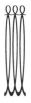

A man's mind, stretched by a new idea, can never go
back to its original dimension.

Oliver Wendell Holmes

It is unfortunate that few people integrate their system and find their
wholeness. That failure, however, does not change the rules of the game
of life or release us from the unrelenting pressure life places on us to
force our growth. It only means that the consciousness we fail to develop
in this lifetime is the consciousness we must develop in our next lifetime.
Death does not end the soul's demand for growth or resolve our lack of
integration and our failure to find our real self. Death is but a timeout,
a rest stop in the long journey of the soul.

The Pace of Evolution

Since most people are not focused on their integration and internal development, their growth proceeds at a glacial pace. One of the critical
functions to fall within the scope of The Law of Consequences (Karma),
is the pace of our individual evolution. The Law of Consequences insures
that our life momentum is proportionate to our consciousness and our
actions. If we don't take action to confront and defeat our toxicity and
integrate our system, the Law of Consequences will keep the karmic cycle active in our life. The repetition of karmic patterns provides a strong
brake to building positive life momentum. Instead of moving toward
our destiny, we repeat our toxic patterns. As long as the karmic brake is
an active force in our life, our growth cannot be anything but hard and
slow. However, when we clear our toxicity, we also remove the karmic
brake from our lives and are free to build positive life momentum. When

our system is clear of toxicity, our mind is clear to act in our best interests. A clear system, a clear mind, and clear action create accelerating life momentum. When we escape the heavy weight of our karma, our growth is much faster, and our life becomes much more satisfying than it would be otherwise.

Three Karmic Principles

Three karmic principles control much of our life experience.

⤙ *The core concern of the karmic process is the restoration of balance.* When we suffer the pain we once caused someone else, we are being given a critical opportunity to increase our sensitivity to the sufferings of others and to also learn respect for the sanctity of lives other than our own. If we learn from the suffering our past actions have brought upon us, we can restore our balance and complete our karma with respect to that particular issue. If we do not learn from our suffering, our suffering will continue until we do. Once our karma has been set in motion, the only control we have over it is how long it will take us to learn from it.

⤙ *When we strengthen the negative side of our being, we lengthen our evolutionary journey.* Add to our karma, and we may well be adding to the number of lifetimes that are necessary to complete our growth and realize our true identity. Even if we don't add to the number of our lifetimes, we will certainly add to the karmic weight we must work out of our system in this lifetime. The more karmic weight we carry, the more unhappy and lost we will be, and the more the negative side of experience will dominate our lives.

⤙ *When we add to our karma, we slow our life momentum.* The opposite of this karmic principle is also true. When we clear up our unconscious toxicity, our life begins to accelerate. We gain spiritual traction and develop positive life momentum. Our consciousness begins to grow and expand. Our inner light becomes brighter. We begin to get a glimpse of who we really are and experience a greater sense of happiness and inner peace than we had previously known. However, if we still insist on creating more negative karma, none of these positive developments will occur. Upward momentum will wither and fail. Traction will disappear. Inertia will set in. Discouragement and anxiety will become our constant companions and new layers of pain and darkness will obscure the truth of our being.

The sad thing about negative karma is that most of it is utterly unnecessary, a waste of time, energy, and other resources that could be put to more productive uses. Next time, before acting out of spite or reacting impulsively out of anger to hurt another person because they have hurt you, think about the price that you will have to pay one day for your actions. In the end, nothing we do is without consequence.

The wise person knows all this and does good things, building positive momentum to move forward in his life. The foolish person goes on blindly ignoring the Law of Consequences, digging a deeper karmic hole that he will have to climb out of in the future. More often than not, that climb is long and laborious. When we choose to resist the inner imperative to grow, we are choosing to let our karma and our toxicity control our life.

Life Beyond the Physical Plane

Science tells us that nature abhors a vacuum. When we die, we do not turn to dust and bleached bones in the ground. Dust and bones are merely the remains of the body. Our body is the vehicle that houses and transports our soul while we are here on earth. While the remains of the body are ours, those remains are not who we are. This is a crucial distinction. At death, the electromagnetic energy field that contains the spirit/soul/mind is no longer tethered to the physical plane by the physical body. When we die, the invisible silver cord linking the soul to the body is broken, and the soul returns to its home on the astral plane. Where we go in the astral worlds when we leave the body at death depends on how much or how little spiritual light we built into our system while we were here.

In this world, the soul is hidden and clothed in flesh. In the higher worlds, the soul stands revealed in its own light. That light is the real body of the soul. The brighter the light, the more powerful and evolved the soul has become.

THE STORY OF PAULA AND TED

My friend Paula once told me the story of her husband Ted's death. Ted had been in declining health for a long time, and one day he had a heart attack. Paula called 911. The medics arrived quickly and were able to revive him. Paula, of course, was greatly relieved. Ted, however, was not. After he recovered, he scolded Paula.

"Listen," he said in the no nonsense manner that was his trademark, "the next time that happens don't try to bring me back."

"Why Ted?" Paula asked him, a hint of panic in her voice.

"Paula, I was out of my body, experiencing more peace than I ever knew existed. I was in a very bright place. It was so light and so beautiful, better than anything I ever experienced here, I'll tell you that. I'm not afraid to die now. I love you very much, Paula, and I don't want to leave you behind, but my time is coming soon. I know it, and you know it. It won't be much longer. That's just the way it is. You promise to let me go next time, Paula? No more calls to 911?"

"Okay Ted," Paula told him reluctantly. "I promise."

A few months later Ted had another heart attack. This time Paula stilled her panic and remembered her promise. Instead of reaching for the phone, she reached for Ted's hand and held him as he died.

"Alan," she told me years later when she could talk about losing Ted without emotion, "when Ted died, I could see his spirit rise out of him and go up through the ceiling."

"What did it look like?" I asked her.

"It was a long strand of silvery white light," she replied without hesitation.

"And that's not all. When he left his body there was a feeling of deep peace in the room. Knowing that he was at peace made his death a lot easier for me to bear. It also helped me let go of my own fears about dying."

Life is hard and unrelenting, and will always challenge us to grow. As Ted was fond of saying, "That's just the way it is."

Building Life Momentum

We earn access to more internal light and develop a conscious connection to our soul by the manner in which we live our lives. Are we honest? Do we maintain our integrity? Do we respect the rights of others? Can we set aside our personal desires for the good of others? Are we compassionate and kind to those less fortunate than ourselves? Do we help people? Did we ever sacrifice our self-advantage so that someone else might have a better opportunity? Have we grown in our capacity for unconditional love? Have we forgiven those who trespassed against us? Have we cleared our toxicity? Do we know who we really are? If our answers to these questions are in the affirmative, then we are using the Law of Consequences to our advantage and building positive momentum in our life.

Nothing Stays the Same

This is a world of impermanence. It is ruled by change and uncertainty. Nothing here stays the same or lasts forever. We are born into these conditions, conscious to some degree and mortal in the highest degree. We have just enough consciousness to spend most of our life trying to subdue our anxiety by finding a measure of permanence in the world. Sadly, most of us do not yet have enough consciousness to realize that the only real permanence we will ever find in this world is the inner light we build within us while we are here. As we build our light, we grow our soul and pull the power of the Divine down into our lives. One of the great heartbreaks of life is that we all have enough consciousness to struggle and suffer, but most of us do not yet have enough consciousness to find joy and fulfillment.

Abundance

While material abundance is the answer to one set of life's problems, it is not the answer to life's deepest needs. Abundance solves our survival needs and provides the means to manifest our lifestyle choices, allowing us to sustain our lives in a manner of our choosing. It is certainly far better to have abundance than to be mired in poverty, but abundance will not cure our inner hunger for happiness and fulfillment, no matter how many of our desires we are able to fulfill. Abundance by itself will not reveal our identity to us or resolve the internal emptiness that afflicts a large percentage of the world's population. Psychiatrists' couches, after all, are filled with clients who are very successful and very unhappy.

The scientific materialism of the West has always been too one-sided, stressing material success to the detriment of spiritual development. The times we live in are a period of major imbalance. Stress, fear, hatred, and conflict are all at epidemic proportions. This disturbing trend is of immense consequence for the future. If we don't pursue our inner development with the same vigor that we have pursued material success, the tide of negativity may well overwhelm the world.

Winning the Game

Our job is to understand the game of life and play that game to win. Understanding how the Law of Consequences functions will help us win that game on our internal levels. We win when we grow our inner light and realize who we really are. The wise person plays the game for the long term. He is not interested in building karma that may create a short-term personal advantage but carries with it a long-term liability. He knows that the price he will eventually have to pay for that temporary advantage is too high. He is interested in generating more light in his life rather than more darkness. This world is dark enough already. With each dark and reprehensible act, it becomes a more fearful and angry place, where peace and sanity evaporate and acts of continual retribution ratchet up the violence to appalling heights.

Why We Are Here

Earth is the place we must come to in order to heal the splits in our psyche and overcome our separation from the light of our soul. Physical life was never meant to be easy or permanent. It was designed to force our growth. At every step of the way, we must choose between what will help us go forward and what will lead us astray. We can be engines of illumination or generators of karmic pollution. The choices we make will either clarify the light in our soul or increase the karmic weight in our system. We can quicken the pace of our evolution or add to its burdens and length of time. We can rise in the light or sink in the darkness.

When the Divine gave man free will, He also gave man karma so he would have to be responsible for his actions. Nothing is free or without consequence. The price of freedom is letting go of everything we think we are and are not. The game of life was set in stone eons ago. We have no control over its nature, but we do have control over our nature. Beware what kind of player you become in the game of life.

SEAN

Several years ago when my office was in Austin, Texas, I had a client named Sean whom I only saw once. Sean came because his girlfriend had paid for his session in advance and he hated to waste money. Otherwise, he would never have come. He was quite clear on that point.

When Sean's session began, I placed one hand under the base of his spine and my other hand under the base of his skull. As the energy coming through my hands flooded Sean's central nervous system, his eyes opened wide, and he stared at a fixed point on the ceiling. After a long moment of intense concentration, he closed his eyes. He sighed, his face turned ashen gray, and he began to shake his head slowly from side to side. After a few moments, he began shaking all over. Several more minutes passed, and he began to sob. He sobbed for a long time, his sobs becoming deeper and more anguished as he became immersed in his unconscious toxicity. Finally the sobbing stopped, and Sean's body began to vibrate from the top of his head right down to the soles of his feet. He vibrated intensely for several minutes then suddenly became ice cold.

It was the middle of summer, but I had to put two heavy blankets over him. The blankets did little good. The cold was coming out of him, ancient, dead energies that had been frozen in his soul a long time ago. He needed to "thaw out" before those old energies would be cleared completely from his system. The freezing and the shaking continued. After a while longer, he came back to normal consciousness and opened his eyes. He was gray, exhausted, and still quite cold. I gave him more time to get his bearings and then asked him what he had experienced.

He said that when he opened his eyes shortly after the session began, he saw a stream of white light flowing from his forehead, culminating in a white cross on the ceiling. The cross was there for only a moment. When it disappeared, he closed his eyes again. No sooner had he closed his eyes than he found himself in another lifetime that was quite foreign to him and to which he could not relate.

Sean had seen himself as a slave in ancient Egypt, one of thousands pulling stones slowly across the desert. He was in a long line of slaves pulling a thick rope attached to a large stone. There were many over-seers keeping the slaves organized and working at full capacity. If a slave appeared to weaken or give less than his full effort, an overseer would pull him out of the line and whip him, often quite severely. Many slaves were whipped to death.

As Sean watched the scenes unfolding in his mind's eye, an angry overseer pulled a woman out of her place in the line of slaves just ahead of him. He whipped her until her blood stained the sand around her feet. She collapsed and soon died. Sean distinctly remembered showing no emotion at the time of her death. He knew that if he were to show emo-tion, he would bring the overseer down on him, and he would suffer a similar fate. So he bottled whatever emotion he felt at the death of this woman and continued to pull the rock along the sand with the other slaves in his contingent as if nothing had happened.

Now that he had released the emotion frozen in his soul more than twenty-five hundred years ago, he knew without a doubt that the dead woman had been his wife. The fact that his grief was more than two thousand years late was not important now. The only thing that mat-tered was that he was finally able to feel his ancient wounding and free himself from it's dominance in his life.

Sean's Unconscious Governing Beliefs

The legacy of that ancient experience had been a heavy karmic anchor in Sean's subconscious and had chained him to failure and obscurity in his present life. That karmic anchor contained two unconscious beliefs that controlled his life. The first unconscious belief was the notion that if you loved someone they would die, as his wife had died in ancient Egypt. The second unconscious belief was the notion that it was dangerous to be seen by those in power in the light of day. If you stayed out of sight you would avoid punishment and survive.

In alignment with his unconscious governing beliefs, yet without any conscious knowledge of those beliefs, Sean found employment as a bartender, working in the shadows of a darkened bar, and indulged in a series of one-night stands that were meaningless, devoid of love, and went nowhere. In terms of his unconscious governing beliefs, Sean was successful. He wasn't seen and he stayed alive. He didn't love anyone, and no one died. Of course, his success at staying alive and having no emotional connection with anyone held no conscious satisfaction for him so he took recreational drugs daily to mask his pain. While he had no conscious awareness about his predicament, he was the prisoner of unconscious governing beliefs more than two millennia old.

Within a few months of releasing the trauma and grief of that lifetime, Sean's life totally changed. He was freed from living under the spell of his unconscious governing beliefs. He got a sales job with a prestigious high-tech company, gave up drugs and meaningless sex, and became engaged to a wonderful girl he cared for deeply. By clearing one ancient lifetime from his system about which he had had absolutely no awareness, Sean was able to elevate his life in a very fast, yet natural way and gain his freedom from the past.

MICHAEL

The distant past can also have severe repercussions on our physical well-being. Michael came to a one day workshop I held at Michigan State University in the mid nineteen eighties. He was one of the first people to get on a healing table. The healing energy in the room that day was very powerful, and when the people in his group laid their hands on him, the healing energy that came through their hands surged through his system immediately. His eyes closed in response to the energy, and he became very peaceful, but not for long. A moment later, he was screaming and sweating, arms flailing, legs kicking the table as hard as they could. For a mild mannered and slightly built man, there was a tremendous rage bottled up in his system. His emotional release went on for some time. Finally, his catharsis ended, and he became very quiet and peaceful again. When he opened his eyes a while later, I asked him to tell me what he had experienced.

He said that when his whole body filled with bright white light in the beginning of the session, he felt peaceful and very happy. However, that feeling lasted only a minute. Without any rational reason that he could name, he found himself thrown back in time to the Inquisition, where he relived an experience he would have rather avoided. He was a priest accused of heresy and ordered by the Inquisition tribunal to recant. He refused to do so, knowing that he had committed no crime. He was tortured, then castrated, and left to die in a pool of his own blood.

After Michael shared his experience I asked him two questions. How was he feeling now, and did he see any connection between that lifetime and this one? He said that he was feeling incredibly light and peaceful, and yes, there was a definite connection between that life and this one. Three years earlier he had been diagnosed with testicular cancer and had had one of his testicles removed. Now he realized that all the rage and hatred from being castrated some five hundred years earlier had been stored in his system and reappeared in the same physical location in this lifetime. That unhealed rage created his cancer and caused him to be partially castrated again. His karmic rage had drawn the past to him and repeated the trauma again.

After Michael got off the table, he asked me if he could call his wife and have her come to the afternoon session. I told him that would be fine. His wife was an attractive and pleasant woman, but rather overweight. During her session on the table that afternoon, she cried for a long time before she became peaceful like Michael had earlier in the day.

When her experience was complete, I asked her what had occurred. She told me that as soon the energy began flowing into her system, she found herself in another lifetime where she had been a young Indian girl in a South American village high in the Andes. There wasn't enough food in the village, and she was always hungry. She eventually died of starvation as a child. I asked her if that experience had affected her in this lifetime. She said that she was still always hungry, no matter how much food she ate. Craving food had been a life long constant for her.

A few months later I received a call from Michael's wife. She was eager to share what had happened in the intervening weeks since she had attended the workshop. Her constant craving for food was gone, and she had lost over twenty pounds without trying.

Clearing our system of its impediments, its karma, and its toxicity is one of the most important tasks of our life. Growth and evolution are not a function of instant gratification, but one of internal purification. Purification is not an immediate and superficial process, but a deliberate and deep one. It not only takes time, but it is also worthy of the time it takes.

Toward the end of his life, the great poet T.S. Eliot crafted a volume of four brilliant poems on life, meaning, and suffering that he entitled, *The Four Quartets.* In the Four Quartets, Eliot wrote that, "... all will be well, and all manner of things will be well, by the purification of the motive in the ground of our beseeching."

When we finally purify our own motives by clearing our karma, things will change for the better, not only in this lifetime, but in all lifetimes yet to come.

eight THE TASKS OF INTEGRATION

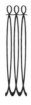

The trouble with the world is that the stupid are
cocksure and the intelligent are full of doubt.
Bertrand Russell

Not everything that can be counted counts, and not
everything that counts can be counted.
Albert Einstein

When we have met the three goals of the Elimination Zone, it is time to move on to the next zone of growth, Integration. The five tasks of the Integration Zone build upon our previous success in clearing the toxicity from our system. Without clearing that toxicity, we cannot move forward to the next zone of growth.

The five primary tasks of the integration zone are to:

- *Establish effective boundaries.*

- *Stand up for one's self.*

- *Build an inner center.*

- *Create a healthy ego by aligning the ego with the soul.*

- *Serve the greater good.*

While more toxicity will inevitably surface as we continue our march into the light in the Integration Zone, discharging that toxicity will not be our primary concern, as it was in the Elimination Zone. Rather than deliberately searching for toxic material, we will deal with it as it arises.

What makes the surfacing of more hidden material inevitable is that, as we go forward, we will pull down more light from above into our system. This new infusion of spiritual light will expose whatever toxicity may be still lurking deep within us and did not arise during our experience in the Elimination Zone.

When more toxicity surfaces, it should not be an occasion to fall into depression or to be consumed by a sense of failure that we did not clear all our toxicity earlier. As more toxicity emerges, it is important to remember that every encounter with the darkness remaining in our system is an opportunity to establish greater freedom and generate a brighter internal light. The real message behind the surfacing of more toxic material is simply that we have gained an important opportunity to transform our remaining darkness into light. A positive outcome to that confrontation insures that we will have more integration, power, and freedom than we had before. Every time we clear more darkness from our system, we build more momentum into our life.

A Standard of Perfection

As we move forward it is important to remember that we are not perfect but are, rather, works in progress. To expect to attain a level of absolute completion when we emerge from the elimination phase is unrealistic. To harbor the false hope of absolute completion is to plant the seed of certain discouragement. The only standard of perfection we have to be concerned with is that of increasing our internal radiance. When increasing our radiance is our standard, encountering a toxic layer we have not been aware of is not evidence of our failure. It is an opportunity to further magnify our light.

When the Elimination Zone ends, we will be feeling lighter and more whole. We will have more personal power, and many good things will be starting to percolate under the surface of our lives. With much hard work behind us and new doors beginning to open for us, it might seem as if our work were largely over. That conclusion is both right and wrong. For the most part, the Elimination Zone is over, but our work in the Integration Zone is just beginning.

The Purpose of the Integration Zone

The purpose of the Integration Zone is to stabilize our system, protect our psyche from psychological and emotional exploitation, and guard our energies from being drained by others. In the Integration Zone, we consolidate our strength, develop our self-worth, and focus on building a positive future.

As we enter the Integration Zone, our first task is to establish healthy and effective boundaries. We create effective boundaries when we construct a psychological "line in the sand" that allows us to maintain our wholeness and protect our sense of self. In effect, a boundary is similar to a "Do Not Enter" sign, a warning of what will happen if you trespass. One of the boundaries by which I live has six words: Abuse me, and you lose me.

An effective boundary allows us to be kind, decent, pleasant, and thoughtful most of the time, but when conditions warrant, a good boundary will prod us to have some sting to our voice and a measure of bite to our bark. Teddy Roosevelt put this idea in very succinct language when he said, "Speak softly but carry a big stick."

Being nice all the time will not save us from being exploited or abused. A bully usually picks on someone nice and meek who won't offer much resistance or fight back. That's what makes him a bully. He instinctively knows that the nice, meek person doesn't have good boundaries and is too afraid to stand up for himself. However, when we are whole and in our power, we will be able to establish healthy boundaries that allow us to calibrate our responses to other people's behavior. We will be nice and decent when people are decent to us. When people are abusive or manipulative to us, we will modulate our response accordingly. Instead of being nice and compliant, we will be firm and formidable. A strong boundary requires a strong backbone to defend it.

We should never permit anyone to abuse us. Suffering ongoing abuse destroys our self-esteem and wounds us deeply. Once the shame of being abused is imbedded into our system, it will draw more shaming experiences into our life. If we are to be free of toxic shame in the future, it is important to set clear boundaries and stand up for ourselves.

Self-Defense Strategies

If we were being verbally abused, for example, one of the best ways to stand up and protect ourselves would be to walk away from our antagonist. While walking away takes maturity and self-restraint, it also protects our inner self from being wounded. If we lack the emotional maturity to walk away, we might be tempted to show our strength by engaging our opponent at his game. If we choose the path of engagement, we will only succeed in opening ourselves to more verbal abuse that could escalate into physical violence. Engagement is just what our antagonist wants, and since that is what he wants, we should not give it to him. Let him hold onto his own shame. Our job is not to let him pass his shame on to us. If we were to lose our self-discipline and engage him on his terms that is exactly what would happen. His shame would become our shame. When we react, we fail to protect ourselves.

One of the best ways to enforce a boundary then, is to deprive our antagonist of what he wants. When we do that we hold the power. If we engage him, we give him our power and make ourselves vulnerable to harm. By engaging him, we have invited him to hurt us further. By giving him the opportunity to hurt us, we are sacrificing our well-being in order to defend our ego. A healthy boundary assigns a higher value to our well-being than it does to defending our ego.

However well we craft a boundary, it will be useless to us, unless we are willing to stand up for ourselves and enforce it. As the philosopher, Martin Buber, wrote in the early years of the twentieth century, "If I am not for me, who will be?" The answer to that question is self-evident: no one. There are many things in life that we must do for ourselves. Standing up to protect our integrity is one of them.

The Benefits of Setting Boundaries

There are four major benefits to setting effective boundaries.

> ✦ *The first benefit of having strong boundaries is that they prevent our power from being siphoned off by those who would like to exploit us.* When we stand up for ourselves we are refusing to

let our power be taken from us. I once heard a famous poet being interviewed by Bill Moyers on PBS. During her conversation with Mr. Moyers, she told the story of three men she had dated briefly. Each one wanted to change something they didn't like about her. One liked her but wanted her to change her hair. Another liked her but wanted her to lose weight. A third liked her but wanted her to have cosmetic surgery. By trying to change her, she felt that they were all trying to steal a piece of her soul. However, she wasn't in the business of giving her soul away. If they didn't like her for the person she was, she wasn't about to twist herself into the person they wanted her to be. She dumped each of them in succession, feeling strongly that it was more important to protect her sense of self than to be in a relationship in which she gave away a piece of her soul and allowed someone else to control her. By saying no and walking away from each of these men, she affirmed her identity and increased her personal power. In rejecting these negative attacks on her self-worth, she maintained her boundaries and protected her inner self from being damaged.

ᵜ *The second benefit of setting effective boundaries is that when we stand up for ourselves, we retain our inner center and remain connected to our soul.* At the same time, we frustrate the attempts of our adversary to knock us off balance. If we don't let our adversary's energy penetrate our core, there is nothing we have to clear, and we can continue to move forward. When we stand up for ourselves, we won't lose our inner balance. We will remain whole.

ᵜ *The third benefit of setting effective boundaries is that when we stand up for ourselves, we limit the possibilities of being mistreated, abused, used, or shamed.* We control what is within our power to control. While much of life lies beyond our ability to control it, we are always able to control how we respond to challenging circumstances.

    ↦   *The fourth benefit is that when we set effective boundaries, we build positive life momentum, accelerate our growth, and set the stage to further elevate our consciousness.* Elevation can't occur until we have first stabilized our system, consolidated our power, and developed our inner center.

Building a Pattern of Accomplishment

If we do not learn to stand up for ourselves, old patterns of victimization may continue to plague us and we run the risk of being repeatedly mistreated, used, and shamed. If the chronic recurrence of these patterns occurs, they will siphon off our power and cause further distortions in our psyche. Whatever imbalances we have will become more severe, and the unconscious beliefs that govern much of our experience will become more oppressive.

Fortunately, when we complete our work in the Elimination Zone, most of our imbalances have already been corrected, making it much easier to stand up for ourselves. When we do the right things in the right sequence, taking the next step is always much easier because we are building upon an established pattern of accomplishment. Standing up for ourselves is very different when we have freed ourselves from the victim role than it is when the victim mentality still controls us. In the first case, we have eliminated our toxicity, regained our power, and become whole. In the second case, we are still toxic and powerless, and the inner victim is as self-destructive as ever.

BARBARA

Barbara is a former client from Florida. She is a charming, sophisticated, and intelligent woman in her mid-sixties. Several years ago, Barbara's husband passed away. At the time of his death, she had been married to him for nearly forty years. When she called to arrange a series of telephone consultations, she was certain that she had completed her grieving over her husband's death and that it was no longer an issue in her life.

When Barbara had her first consultation over the phone some

weeks later, I could see that the energy from his death still lingered in her chest and heart. Accordingly, I directed her attention to her chest area and asked her to make guttural sounds as if they were coming out of her heart. When she started to make these non-verbal sounds, I directed the healing energy pouring out of my hands over the phone into her chest. After a few minutes of making half-hearted grunts and sighs and getting nowhere, she wanted to stop. She complained that making these sounds just wasn't lady-like, and didn't feel right.

"Barbara," I said gently, "there's no one here but you and me, and it's okay to feel uncomfortable. It really is. You don't have to be a lady in this context, just someone who wants to heal her life and stop her pain. No one feels very comfortable when they're stirring up their toxicity anyway. For the first time you're stepping out of the box you've been trapped in your whole life. Give yourself a chance to succeed. You'll like how success feels, I promise."

"Okay," she said cautiously. "I'll give it another shot. But how long do I have to make the sounds for?"

She was still obviously in resistance.

"Until a wall inside you breaks," I replied, "and the toxic material that has been sealed off behind that barricade pours out of you. Then you won't have to force the sounds anymore. You won't have to make yourself grunt, sigh, and scream. You'll just erupt. Your unconscious material will rise to meet your conscious mind. In all real healing, the subconscious mind and the conscious mind temporarily become one. When that happens, your conscious mind will be unable to censor and repress your unconscious pain. As the conscious mind and the unconscious material become joined, the pain will just pour out of you until it no longer exists. When the two become one, your toxicity will be ignited. After you complete that specific layer, your conscious and unconscious will separate and return to their normal stations. Only you will be freer, more balanced, and filled with more light."

"That last part is what I'm after. How long will it take before that happens?"

"No one really knows. Hopefully, not long. But it certainly isn't going to happen while we're talking and you're not making the sounds I have asked you to make. Do you think you can go forward now?"

"Yes," she answered resolutely.

We were lucky that first day. The blockage in her heart proved to be very mobile, and it broke easily. Within a matter of minutes the pain rose out of her chest and into her throat. As the toxic energy burst out of its hiding place, the painful emotion it contained flooded her conscious mind. She was no longer in control of herself. What needed to come out of her was stronger than her capacity to control it. She broke down and cried uncontrollably for the rest of the session.

At the end of the session, Barbara noted that this was awfully hard work. She was hoping to feel better, not worse, as she did now. I told her not to worry about how she felt. That was temporary and would pass. The important thing for her to focus on was what had just happened. The toxicity had surfaced, broken, and poured out of her system. Many layers of grief had been cleared in an hour. That was most impressive.

"Processing grief is always hard work," I said. "Nothing about it is easy. No one wants to feel the pain it brings up, and besides, the energy of grief itself is very heavy. That's why processing the psychic *weight* of grief is exhausting. For the next few days you can expect to feel a bit low and tired. The healing energy I channeled into your body is extremely potent and will continue to work on you for several more days. Don't be surprised if you cry and clear more toxic emotion between sessions. That's normal in this work. You'll feel better in a few days."

Her next appointment was a week later. When she called in she reported that she had indeed felt depressed and tired, and had cried for a few days after our first session. I asked her how she felt today. She replied that for the last two days she had been feeling really good and much, much lighter, but now she was afraid to do another session because she didn't want to feel bad again.

I said that I didn't blame her for feeling that way. "No one likes feeling low," I continued, "but the thing to remember is that every time you go through a cleansing experience, and work your way through unconscious toxic emotion, you will tend to feel a bit depleted. Feeling that way is a sign that real healing has taken place. When you recover you will feel lighter, freer, and more energized than before. That's just how the healing process goes. Every layer you peel away opens the way to more inner light, connects you more to your real self, and restores you to more of your personal power. You go through a little to gain a lot. You suffer some sadness and exhaustion that is short-lived, but you gain a happiness and clarity that will be long-lived. As you move forward, your highs will become higher, and your lows will also become higher."

Carrying Karma Forward

"Besides," I continued, "while you might feel out of sorts as you clear the heavy energies of grief from your system, just imagine having to carry that weight forward in your life. When you experienced your grief in its raw and elemental state last week, you felt exactly what you had been carrying around with you for years. It wasn't hidden anymore or hanging over your life like a cloud of low-level depression and unhappiness, poisoning your existence and sapping your spirit of its vitality. Instead, you felt the entire weight of what had been buried in your heart and you embraced it. In choosing to face and clear it, you chose expansion over confinement, happiness over depression, and a better future for yourself. So don't worry about what you may feel in today's session and in the days that follow. Focus instead on where you're going and hope that even more toxic emotion comes out of you today than it did last week. If that should happen, it will only free you more."

That week, more grief did pour out of her, but it was not all related to the death of her husband. Behind the grief of her husband's passing was the sullen grief of her childhood. She had grown up in a cold house with a critical mother and an emotionally absent father. She had never felt safe in expressing her feelings in her family environment. To say what she felt or to stand up for what she wanted was to invite a withering attack from her mother. Her mother regularly shamed and humiliated her, making her feel small, inadequate, unwanted, and unloved. Given her background, it was not surprising that her whole strategy as a child was simply to survive. Her strategy for survival was anchored in pleasing her mother in order to reduce her exposure to more shame and verbal degradation.

↗ When she became an adult, Barbara's childhood strategy of pleasing others did not disappear. It had become too ingrained in her behavior. Although she had a new cast of people to relate to as an adult, the childhood pattern of how she related to them endured. It had become her unconscious governing belief. Her experience of being shamed by her mother had led her to conclude that she was unlovable. If I'm not loveable, her subconscious reasoned, then I have to work extra hard to get people to like me. Instead of trying to please her mother, she now tried to please her husband and sons.

As a result of Barbara's childhood conditioning, she was unable to say how she really felt as a grown woman. She lacked the courage to stand up for herself and express her real needs. Her childhood survival theme of "hide your real feelings and don't rock the boat under any circumstances" had become a constant form of unconscious oppression dominating her adult life. One of the problems in trying to please her own family was that she wasn't getting love and respect from her husband and sons in return. All the giving went one way from her to them. There was nothing coming back to her, except more demands for her to do more things for them. She wasn't being seen or respected for who she was. Underneath it all, she burned with unexpressed resentment, a resentment she could not even admit to herself. She was too focused on being a "lady." In her case, being a lady was a cover for not facing her hidden rage, as well as a way to avoid facing her real feelings.

As her second session progressed, Barbara's tears of grief at her husband's death turned to screams of rage at her mother for her coldness, her lack of love, and her failure to nurture and approve of her daughter. After a time, her rage turned to sobs, as she felt the grief of her childhood shame and humiliation. With her grief came the searing realization that she felt lost in life and had no idea of who she really was. As that insight hit her, Barbara's sobs deepened and a plaintive scream arose from that deep, lost place inside her. The scream started out loud and fierce and long, running slowly out of steam until it became a whisper, then a sound no more. She took a moment, gathered the breath back into her body, and resumed her screaming. As her screams dwindled and died, her sobbing resumed. This time the sobs were soft, low, and rapid, one following after the other in a steady, constant rhythm. When her sobs ended, her body became ice cold and began to vibrate.

The session was now nearly concluded. Barbara was absolutely exhausted. However, I became quite excited for her when she told me that her body was vibrating all over and she was feeling ice cold. These symptoms were important markers in her healing just as they had been for Sean. The coldness that she was feeling represented the melting of the shame and loss of identity that had been frozen inside her as a young child and had plagued her ever since. As long as that frozen energy remained in her core she was powerless to move beyond it. The pattern of trying to please others to get their love would remain intact. Now that frozen energy was melting. It was a moment of great significance for Barbara. It meant that she was no longer trapped in the emotional context of her childhood.

Resetting the Emotional Clock

The rapid vibrating of Barbara's body was her system's method of resetting her emotional clock and accelerating the energies in her emotional body so that they might catch up to her chronological age. When her body stopped vibrating, one part of her would no longer be in its mid-sixties, while the other part of her stayed stuck in shame at age six. Now her chronological age and her emotional life would be synchronized at the same level of maturity.

As a child, she always had to be vigilant and on guard, constantly looking over her shoulder for the criticism that was sure to come her way if she dared to step out of the box into which her circumstances had forced her. She had had no choice but to be what someone else had wanted her to be. Now the compulsion to please, and the fear, shame, need, and rage that had been stuck in her body since early childhood were cleared from her system. She had ventured outside the box of her childhood conditioning and would never be the same again.

The "endure to survive" theme that had dominated her childhood and sabotaged her adult years would no longer control her. She was no longer firmly entrenched on the path of most resistance. Barbara's healing experience taught her that change could happen at any age and that it was indeed possible to teach an old dog new tricks.

Signs of Transformation

The first outward sign of Barbara's growth occurred in an interaction with an old friend. For many years, she had considered this particular woman her best friend. Yet this woman consistently irritated and upset her. Until now, Barbara had never really examined the source of that irritation. She had just thought that her feelings were due to a hidden flaw within herself, rather than to a problem with her friend. Instead of being able to look objectively at her friendship, she had internalized her feelings and blamed herself. The shame that her mother had instilled in her as a child had created low self-esteem and led her to blame herself whenever anything went wrong. Now that she was clearer and more confident in herself, she realized that the irritation she experienced whenever she was with this woman occurred because her friend routinely used her and treated her dismissively.

The next time her friend called and said something that upset her, Barbara told her exactly how she felt about being treated in this manner. The woman then became very nasty, berating Barbara and treating her even more contemptuously. Barbara was not about to put up with that kind of treatment ever again. She told the woman that their friendship was over and hung up the phone. When she told me about it a few days later she was still feeling very proud of herself and couldn't believe that she felt no remorse.

"Why should you?" I asked her. "All you did was tell her the truth."

"I know," she said, "but the old Barbara would have felt terrible and scared and done everything under the sun to put it back together. Now I couldn't care less. I feel terrifically empowered. I never knew I could feel so good about myself."

"Think about what happened with this woman," I continued.

"There's more here than meets the eye. This was a very significant moment in your growth. Your friend was very much like your mother. They shared the same essential characteristic. By standing up to her you also symbolically stood up to your mother. Congratulations are in order. You just broke the unconscious governing belief that had ruled your life."

The same need to stand up for herself began to occur in all of Barbara's important relationships. A few weeks after telling her former friend the truth, her sons called. They wanted her to come over and watch the Super Bowl with them and their wives and bring some food with her. She told them that she hated sports and wasn't about to be used for free food. If they wanted to see her, it would have to be something she liked to do, and they could supply the food. After all, they were now grown men.

Their reaction surprised her. She expected them to be very upset, but they were not upset at all. They fully agreed with her position and apologized for their behavior. Since that conversation, their relationship is on an entirely different plane. They now have a mother they respect and are proud of. They even cook her dinner.

For Barbara, the lesson in standing up for herself was clear and simple. She lost those people who were not her real friends, made new ones to replace them who were much more positive than the old ones, and gained the respect of those that really mattered to her. In terms of her growth, her losses were really gains. She lost what didn't matter and was no longer relevant to her growth. By rejecting negative people she affirmed her own self-worth, increased her personal power, and protected her core just as the famous writer interviewed by Bill Moyers had done.

Working From the Inside Out

Barbara's progress, from eliminating her toxicity to setting effective boundaries and enforcing them, once again illustrates the importance of doing things in the right sequence. Since she had already cleared her toxicity, she didn't really have to think about setting boundaries or developing strategies to enforce them. She just did what she had to do in the normal course of her daily life without realizing until later what it was she had really done. Barbara didn't fret or agonize over taking action. She didn't force anything. She didn't have to read a bunch of self-help books, or try to manage a difficult situation. She didn't try to control or manipulate every facet of her life. She just acted from the *inside out*, allowing her intuition to lead her into action.

Most people haven't cleared their toxicity in the way that Barbara has, and so they are stuck trying to cope with ongoing, persistent problems, rather than transforming the landscape of their subconscious and being in a position of wholeness in their lives. Without that transformation, the average person's only remedy is to try to force his conscious will on his unconscious toxicity and its governing beliefs. This is working from the *outside in*. When we try to impose our conscious will on an unhealed subconscious, our chances of success are minimal. In most cases, working from the outside in is really a prescription for frustration and failure.

FRANK

During my years in Austin, Texas, one of my clients was a quiet and melancholy man named Frank. Frank had been in the Merchant Marine for nearly forty years. At the time of our meeting, he was the second mate on a large cargo ship and had traveled all over the world in his time at sea.

When Frank started to work with me, he was in a pretty bad way. His third wife had recently left him while he had been away at sea. She had drained his bank accounts, sold his car, coin collection, and home furnishings, and headed north to Indiana. When Frank came home from his voyage, all he had left was the house. There was virtually nothing in it.

Despite Frank's cool and non-emotional exterior, his underlying bitterness was quite apparent. We soon worked out a routine. When he was between voyages, he would come up to Austin from his home in Houston and work several times a week with me. At first, little happened in those initial sessions. Frank just soaked up the energy and felt great. He got to thinking that all he had to do was lie on my table and he'd feel light and happy for days.

I told him that with any luck, his experience of getting high would soon go away. He thought I was kidding. Why would I want him to feel any different from the way he was now feeling? Wasn't the goal of healing to feel better? Sure, I replied, but to feel better on a long-term basis, you have to confront and clear your toxicity. Otherwise, all you're doing is getting a temporary energy high and becoming addicted to being with me so you can get that high. That's not the goal here.

"What is the goal then?" he asked.

"The goal is to transform your toxicity, become clear and whole, and outgrow your need of me."

Then I told him that only people who were not connected to their toxic content got high at first. In my terminology, he was a category three. When he got wired to his pain and shame all that would change. If he kept coming, he would soon begin to feel all the dense and sluggish energy that was stuffed inside his body. Then he wouldn't feel so good, but not to worry, I continued. That was real progress.

He gave me a funny look when I said that. I don't think he knew whether to believe me or not. The following week, after one of his daily sessions, Frank was standing in line at the supermarket when his body began to vibrate without prior warning. He had no idea what was going on, but he was smart enough to get back to his motel room as soon as he could. By the time he got to his room, Frank was really shaking. Nothing remotely like that had ever happened to him before. Little did he know that the toxic energy in his system was becoming mobile. That's what his shaking was about. He was about to burst. He just didn't know it. He collapsed on his bed, fell asleep immediately, and slept for two hours.

The next week, a lot of highly toxic material surfaced from his childhood. Frank didn't cry or scream. He didn't break wide open like most other people did. His deep reserve and shame wouldn't permit it. In place of a complete catharsis, the internal pressure formed by the mobilized energy rumbling around inside him forced a kind of confession from his lips. He shared his secrets grudgingly. Brutal, stark memories from his childhood surfaced. His mother had been an alcoholic. She was mean when she wasn't drinking and cruel when she was. She resented being married and having children and never let Frank and his siblings forget it.

When he was a child, he often went without food. Sometimes all he had to eat in a day was a small bowl of puffed wheat in the morning before he went to school. Around the age of ten, he remembered his mother screaming at him in a drunken fury that he was so ugly no woman would ever want him. That remark scarred him deeply. Several times during his childhood, she abandoned the family, leaving them at home in the islands while she went to live on the mainland by herself. His father wasn't much better. He was distant, uncommunicative, and verbally abusive.

Frank grew up with little physical security and even less love. The arc of his emotional life as a child was narrow and limited, framed by uncertainty and insecurity at one extremity and by shame and abuse at the other. When he reached the age of eighteen, he left home and went to sea, hoping to start a new life and put his nightmare behind him. At the time he was a depressed kid with a big inferiority complex, too scared to talk to people he didn't know. He had escaped from his mother but not from her toxic influence. She was to cast a long, heavy shadow over his life, no matter where he went or whom he was with.

When I met him some forty years later, he was still a depressed man with a big inferiority complex and still scared to talk to people he didn't know. His relations with women had been a disaster. Nearly every woman he had gotten involved with had hurt and abandoned him. One of his wives had even told him before she left him that he was too ugly to be with. These women were all different in appearance and personality from one another, but they had one vital trait in common. Each of them, without exception, did to him what his mother had done to him. They mocked and belittled him. They shamed him, and they left him.

His mother was dead, decaying bones in a wooden box under six feet of heavy earth on an island a few thousand miles away, but she still owned him. Her face was their face. Their words were her words. Her feelings toward him were their feelings for him. Wherever he went, he drew women to him who were her reflection.

It was a good thing that Frank's conscious intention to succeed in this work was very strong. As a category three, his subconscious toxicity was concrete and not at all ready to give up its controlling interest in his life. Thankfully, after several months, my work with him was finally accelerating. He was now vibrating after each consultation. He learned quickly that he had an hour after each session before the vibrating would start. Then he would feel very tired and need to sleep. During that down time his system processed the toxic energy that had been mobilized earlier. He would have strange dreams. Sometimes his body would feel like it was burning up. At other times it would feel ice cold. The next day there would be more memories for him to talk about.

I never forced it with Frank or tried to make him open up more completely than he could at the time. I knew he was giving it everything he had. I couldn't ask for more.

As our sessions advanced and Frank's toxicity continued to clear, his life began to change in very dramatic ways. He was promoted from second mate to first mate. A short time later he was made captain. He hadn't sought these promotions. They just came to him. After a few tours of duty as a captain, he was recognized as the best master in the fleet and during the Desert Storm campaign of 1991, he was assigned to take classified military cargo to Europe for the U.S. forces massing in the Arabian Gulf.

Every time Frank accepted an opportunity for advancement, he broke the mold in which he had been cast in as a child. By accepting these promotions, he was standing up to his childhood conditioning that said he would always be a failure and stepping into a new sense of himself.

A Negative Feedback Loop

For most of his life Frank had been caught in a negative feedback loop. His poor self-image had been continually reinforced by negative life experiences. As long as that feedback loop existed, he was caught in a suffocating bind of his own making. Now however, the opportunities for advancement that came his way were proof that the negative feedback loop no longer existed. Good things were finally happening to him. New success was being built on the foundation of previous success. Reality was giving him a steady stream of positive feedback. The inner victim that had controlled his life for so long, buried him in deprivation and created the negative feedback loop had been defeated at last.

During the time Frank was in Europe, I was conducting daylong workshops for my advanced clients. These workshops were held once a month and helped my clients accelerate their growth by going even deeper into their unconscious material. When Frank returned, I invited him to the next workshop. He was happy to be included.

There were a large number of women in attendance at that month's workshop. I introduced them all to Frank, who was the only first timer there. What happened during that day amazed me. All, and I mean all, of these women took to Frank immediately. They each wanted him to work on them. They couldn't get over how much heat and healing energy came out of his hands. When it was Frank's turn to get on the table, they all wanted to work on him. They could all sense he needed female approval, and they wanted to make sure he got it. They weren't moved by a sense of pity to work on him. They were genuinely attracted to him. It was a breakthrough moment for Frank, a clear indication that he had overcome his mother's cruel shadow and his real light was now shining. He was now pulling in positive and wholesome women. His mother would haunt him no longer. After that first experience, Frank always came to these monthly workshops when he was not at sea. When he wasn't there, the women missed the hell out of him.

About a year later Frank was asked by his union to go to Washington and lobby Congress on their behalf. He was shocked but very proud of the honor shown him and scared to death to go to the Capitol. I told him to forget about his fear and just do it. He had nothing to lose. It would be a great experience. However, he wasn't so sure about that. Somewhere inside him still lurked the Frank who was too frightened to talk to strangers.

"Look," I told him. "If you can command a large crew on a huge cargo ship going half way around the world, you can certainly sit down in a cushy office and talk to a congressman one on one. Your peers obviously hold you in high esteem and think you're the man for the job. I think it's high time you thought the same way about yourself."

Frank just looked at me warily and grunted.

It took him some time to adjust to the idea, but in the end Frank went and had a great time. He discovered that he really enjoyed talking to Congressmen and Senators. It did great things for his self-esteem. Frank was now a changed man. His determination to grow and his willingness to step into new possibilities that were both foreign to his experience and larger than his self-concept gave him something he had never had before, self-confidence.

It's Never Too Late

The cases of Frank and Barbara hold up hope for all of us. It's never too late to become who you were always meant to be. Barbara was in her mid sixties when she began this work, Frank in his late fifties. In both cases, when they cleared the toxicity from their systems, the next steps in their growth evolved in a natural and clear way. They didn't have to exert a great deal of effort or willpower to try and make things happen. Instead, the things that needed to happen to accelerate their growth found them. All they had to do was stand up for themselves and rise to the occasion.

Barbara stood up for herself by rejecting the negative attacks that were intended to demean her and claimed her self-respect instead. When she stood up for herself, she found that she could laugh and be happy. Frank stood up for himself by coming out of his shell. He stopped hiding from life and was finally seen as the competent, responsible, and highly intelligent person he really was.

Barbara furthered her growth and consolidated her inner center by *rejecting the negative* that had dominated her life since her early childhood. In standing up for herself she broke the last vestiges of control, as well as the accompanying emotional deprivation, that her childhood conditioning had exerted over her. Frank achieved the same objectives by accepting *the positive* in his life. He stood up for himself by stretching beyond the limits of his past negative experience. He accepted his promotions. He went to Washington, and he allowed loving women into his life.

Barbara and Frank's methods of standing up for themselves, while diametrically different, served the same ends. Both strategies allowed them to put the toxic shame that had dominated their childhoods behind them. Barbara found her strength in standing up for herself and expressing her feelings. Frank found his self-respect in accepting his professional opportunities and his self-worth in accepting unconditional love. By accepting love from decent, strong, and compassionate women, he proved his mother wrong. He was loveable after all.

Addiction and Powerlessness

Barbara's experience in standing up for herself illustrates yet another important truth. *We can't find happiness when we give away our power.* To be happy, we must have our personal power and maintain our emotional balance.

Those who habitually give away their power are in danger of developing an addictive personality. Having effective boundaries and standing up for ourselves is one of the only safeguards we possess in protecting our power. In contrast, the addictive person has few healthy boundaries. He turns to substance abuse, drugs, alcohol, sex, or other behaviors to replace his loss of power and numb his feelings of toxic shame and the deep sense of inadequacy that accompanies his shame. While addictive behavior may temporarily suppress feelings of self-hatred and low self-esteem, they can never resolve deep-seated emotional problems.

In masking his pain with drugs, alcohol, and sex, the addict only amplifies that pain. By giving away his power, the addict intensifies his anguish. By refusing to face his pain, he unwittingly places himself in a destructive psychological bind. Whatever he flees from becomes larger and more powerful than he is. Whatever is more powerful than he is owns him, becoming the driving force in his life. When that happens, his power is no longer his. It has been transferred to what he fears most and adamantly refuses to face.

The addict, then, has no access to any positive aspect in his psyche. His only thought is to flee from the burden of his life and the weight of responsibility for his growth by making himself *less* conscious. What the addict fails to realize is that the only way to resolve his problems is to become more conscious, not less. However, becoming conscious takes work and commitment, and the addict has no interest in working on himself. While he may not know it, his ultimate goal is self-destruction. He is thoroughly immersed in his negative ego and totally ensconced in the role of victim.

Facing Fear

Fortunately, consciousness can be transformed from any context. We get real when we face our unconscious toxic content. It is the only way we have to regain our power. The addict can alter his path to self-destruction by facing what he fears most. That is the only way he will regain his power. While the secret of what he must do is simple, entering the Elimination Zone is often a formidable undertaking. In the beginning of the journey, moving toward our fear intensifies that fear.

The antidote to fear is courage. In the context of personal evolution, courage means that we have decided to move forward and are willing to feel uncomfortable in order to escape where we have been. That's what Barbara and Frank both did. Courage means we are willing to take a risk in order to be free of an untenable situation. In the case of the addict, courage means that he is willing to sacrifice the habitual and the destructive, the negative comfort zone that he is used to, for a chance at health and redemption.

For the addict, the road home to his real self and his true nature is not a mystery. Its requirements are few. He has to want to do it. Then he has to choose to do it. Then he has to do it.

What the addict has to do to right his boat, we have to do to right ours. The addict's situation is only more desperate, urgent, and extreme than is our own. The difference between an addict and a normal person is but a matter of degree. We may be in different boats, but we still have to sail on the same sea of consciousness.

At some point in life everyone confronts the same question. Are we going to face ourselves and go forward, or are we going to avoid that confrontation, resist our growth, and run in place for the rest of our lives?

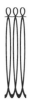

If you've opened your loving to God's love, you're
helping people you don't know and have never met.

Rumi

No man resolved to make the most of himself can spare
time for personal contention. Still less can he afford to
take all the consequences, including the vitiating of his
temper and loss of self-control.

Abraham Lincoln

How much more grievous are the consequences of anger
than the causes of it.

Marcus Aurelius

By eliminating their toxic content, setting boundaries, and standing up for themselves, Barbara and Frank built healthy egos from the ashes of negative ones. What distinguishes a negative ego from a healthy ego is the relationship that each ego level has with the soul.

The negative ego is a closed system, determined to have no further relationship with the soul whatsoever. It sees the soul as its major competitor for power within the psyche. It is threatened by the soul's connection to the eternal light of the spirit. It does not want that light to illuminate the psyche because the negative ego is afraid the light will reveal the hidden darkness and toxicity that are the source of its power. Since the negative ego is dominated by fear, it will go to great lengths to protect its franchise and maintain its control.

The negative ego's primary interest does not lie in serving the person whose system it rules. It is only interested in protecting its host in order to sustain its own existence. This is not an act of generosity, but one of self-interest. The negative ego knows full well that it is as mortal as the body of its host. If its host were to die, it would no longer exist.

The negative ego with its fear, self-absorption, antagonism toward the soul, and concerns about its own survival, has no interest in the growth and evolution of the person within whom it exists. Neither is it interested in helping its host discover his true identity or find his true purpose. Conscious evolution requires the presence of the soul, and the negative ego is fully committed to denying that presence. Since the negative ego's goals are antagonistic to the true goals of the person, it is neither friend nor ally to the person it is supposed to serve.

With its primary orientation organized around its own survival concerns, the negative ego is not interested in growth or integration, but rather, in power and control. Power and control are its solution to the fear that lies hidden at its core. If the person it rules chose to bring down the eternal light and evolve, instead of chasing one desire after another in a futile race for fulfillment, the negative ego would eventually die. Turning toward the light terrifies the negative ego. It knows that it can only achieve its goals of survival and power by misdirecting the person it is supposed to be protecting from further trauma. Its mission is to keep that person in the dark about his darkness, not to usher him into the light.

The Healthy Ego

The healthy ego is just the opposite. It is an open system. It wants to do all it can to help the soul achieve maximum influence in the psyche. It is interested in promoting the growth and evolution of the person it serves. It is a true ally and partner in the pursuit of that growth. It knows it can accelerate its host's growth and evolution by merging with the soul and letting the soul be the ultimate authority in the psyche. It knows instinctively that when that merger occurs it will strengthen every aspect of the psyche, produce a higher level of systemic integration, and widen its host's awareness.

It also knows that as the evolutionary process goes forward from the Integration Zone and enters the Elevation Zone, it will undergo another upgrade, or death experience. The healthy ego, unlike the negative ego, is not afraid of its own death, because it has died once already when making the transition from the Elimination Zone to the Integration Zone. When it died as the negative ego, it was transformed and freed from the chains of unconscious toxicity that bound it in fear and separation.

The healthy ego, unlike the negative ego, seeks continued growth and transformation. It understands that as more light enters and integrates the system of its host, the freer and happier it will be. When the ego is upgraded by the influx of spiritual light, all aspects of the individual's system become freer and brighter. As the ego goes, so goes the individual. The key to personal evolution is to shift the ego toward the pole of the soul and spirit.

The healthy ego is no longer worried about its survival, and no longer dominated by fear. Its goals are no longer antagonistic to the goals of the inner person. Instead, they are the same. The healthy ego is learning to move in harmony with the soul. Where the soul leads, the healthy ego wants to follow.

Ego States and Toxicity

We can find the secret to the great disparity in viewpoint, values, and purpose that exists between the negative ego and the healthy ego in the relationship each level of the ego has with the unconscious toxic content of its host. In the case of the negative ego, the unconscious toxicity in its host's system has not been processed. In the case of the healthy ego, it has. Consequently, the negative ego is built on the foundation of its host's toxic content, while the healthy ego is constructed on the absence of that content. Unprocessed content is crucial to the negative ego's existence. It imbues the negative ego with power and provides it with a mandate to protect its host from further harm.

A critical component of that unprocessed toxicity is the victim mentality. If someone has been hurt, abused, or shamed and has not cleared those experiences from his system, the role of the victim will be present in his psyche, no matter how unconscious or well hidden that role may be. The inner victim is always angry and always blames someone else for its difficulties. Until the person chooses to take responsibility for what has happened in his life, the inner victim will always stop his growth. Growth is just not possible until one takes full responsibility for the weight of his life.

The Inner Victim

By constantly blaming other people for his difficulties, the inner victim makes a costly mistake. What he fails to comprehend is that in blaming others for his problems, he not only renders himself powerless, but also transfers what power he has left to his adversary. The unconscious transfer of power makes the victim less than who he really is and at the same time, makes his adversary more than who he really is.

Two things happen when the victim unconsciously transfers his power to his adversary and neither result is good. First, it makes him feel even more victimized than he did before he unconsciously transferred his power to his adversary. Second, it inflames him with more hatred toward his adversary. Both results widen the gulf that separates the victim from other people and deepens his shame. When the victim transfers his power he expands his sense of victimization. As long as he lets the victim state exist inside him, he can only move in one direction, down into darkness, and away from the light of the soul and spirit. The only thing the victim mentality ever succeeds in doing is making the individual into even more of a victim.

When Toxicity Becomes Radioactive

The relationship between toxic content and the victim mentality makes that toxicity highly magnetic and powerful, almost radioactive. The resultant combination attracts an ever increasing stream of toxic situations into the person's life. These new situations will incline the person polarized by his negative ego to react negatively, like a victim, to perceived threats to his survival, thus causing even more imbalances and fragmentation to his system.

In essence, there is a great irony at work in the primary mission of the negative ego. Instead of protecting its host from more traumatic incidents, the negative ego attracts more traumatic events to him. That is fine with the negative ego, for in adding to its host's traumas, the negative ego increases its power over the host's psyche. While a toxic system does not help the person who must live within the constraints of that toxicity, it does help the negative ego project its power and keep the soul at bay. The negative ego is shrewd and calculating. It knows that the more toxic material there is in its host's system, the less opportunity the host's soul will have to exert its influence and help the person grow.

As noted earlier, the negative ego does not have a death wish. It protects the toxic content in its host system because that toxicity is the source of its power and existence. Its secret mission, as opposed to its primary mission, is to keep the person focused on outward pursuits and dominated by an endless stream of desires. By keeping its host focused on chasing after a stream of desires, the negative ego diverts him from turning within, taking responsibility for his toxicity, and consciously evolving. By keeping its host focused on the external pursuit of happiness, the negative ego insures both its own continuity and its position of power.

Elimination and the Healthy Ego

The healthy ego, by contrast, has already gone through the Elimination Zone. It has turned away from the distraction and glamour of desire and turned inward to confront and clear the unconscious toxicity in its system. In facing its fears it has faced them down. Instead of dissipating its power by turning outward, it is integrating and re-owning its power by moving inward. In moving inward, it is building a positive center of power. Since the healthy ego has cleared the toxicity in its system, it is no longer dominated by the victim mentality and is free to finally develop a clearer sense of self.

As the ego evolves, we evolve. The healthy ego was once the negative ego. The transformation of the negative ego begins when the individual decides he has had enough frustration, emptiness, and suffering; when he admits that desire and denial do not work and can never fulfill their promise to satisfy him; when he sees that it is time to face himself, look within, and clear whatever toxic content he may find there.

The conscious, deliberate engagement with one's unconscious toxicity marks the beginning of the negative ego's death spiral. That confrontation weakens the desire nature and brings healing to the inner victim. As the negative ego is thrown into the spiritual fire of the Elimination Zone, it is slowly purified, refined, and reborn as the healthy ego. Where the negative ego nurtures the darkness and pursues its own separate goals of domination and control, the healthy ego embraces the soul and is eager to pursue the true goals of the individual, growth and evolution.

The Four Principles of Ego Development

The negative ego then, is based on four fundamental factors. These factors are:

-๑   *Unprocessed toxicity.*

-๑   *Self-hatred and the victim mentality.*

-๑   *An innate sense of fear and powerlessness, which often translates into the need to dominate one's relationships with other people.*

-๑   *An unwavering intention to keep the soul isolated from the conscious mind and ego.*

The healthy ego, on the other hand, is happy to grant the soul access to the psyche. It is not interested in distancing itself from the soul, but in closing the gap with the spirit. The healthy ego is also built on four factors, but these factors are very different from those comprising the negative ego. The four factors that contribute to a healthy ego are:

-> *Cleared toxicity.*

-> *Self-respect and a healthy boundary system.*

-> *The ability to love other people, appreciate and acknowledge them for who they are.*

-> *A strong commitment to unite the soul with the conscious mind and ego.*

A healthy ego starts with a clear subconscious. There is no inner victim, no self-hatred, and no tendency toward self-destruction in the healthy ego. Instead, the healthy ego is continually building and expanding its self-respect. Self-respect grows with the ability to reach out and create healthy relationships based on affection and mutual respect. Self-respect is reinforced when we stand up for ourselves. Self-respect flourishes when we are able to give and receive love. Sharing the energy of unconditional love expands and strengthens us. People with a healthy ego instinctively understand that when they wholeheartedly acknowledge another person's talents, gifts, and contributions, they are indirectly acknowledging their own sense of self.

The ability to wholeheartedly support and recognize someone else is only possible when our system has been drained of its toxicity. If we are free of envy, jealousy, pettiness, and vindictiveness, we won't feel threatened by someone else's success or see that person's good fortune as our personal loss. However, until we clear the toxic emotion from our system and learn to set effective boundaries, we will find ourselves caught in a closed system where the tendency will be to do exactly that.

Closed Systems

A closed system is one in which we believe there is a limited amount of power, success, money, attention, or access available to us. When we invest our consciousness in the belief of limitation, someone else's success becomes our loss, and we feel diminished by their accomplishment.

There are three key themes in closed systems thinking that have a strong impact on our behavior. These three themes are an overriding belief in limitation, an overwhelming tendency to take things personally, and an ever-increasing sense of victimization. In a closed system, we end up feeling wounded and victimized by things that in reality have little or no relationship to us.

As an example, let us imagine a closed system involving two adult sisters who are both married. The older sister has two beautiful and bright children who do well in school, have many friends, and are popular with their respective peer groups. The younger sister has one child who takes drugs, gets failing grades, and is a loner with few friends.

The younger sister has been jealous of her older sibling since they were little children. Over the years her jealousy has hardened into hatred. While success comes easily to her older sister, it comes rarely to her. The same pattern of success and failure that has complicated the sisters' relationship with one another has taken root in the lives of their children. The older sister's children are far more successful and better adjusted than is the younger sister's son.

Jealousy and Competition

The younger sister's jealousy causes her to see everything that happens in her life in terms of competition with her sister. She takes everything personally, even when it has nothing to do with her directly. Every new success of her older sister's family wounds her deeply. Every new failure of her son, every bad grade, every run-in with authority, deepens her anguish. She has always seen her older sister as a winner and herself as a failure. No matter what she does to pull even or go ahead, she knows she is doomed to fail. No matter how hard she pushes herself to outdo her sister, she knows deep down that she will continue to lose. With every perceived loss, her sense of victimization grows.

Exactly who is responsible for her anguish? Is it her sister's fault, as she would like to believe? Does her sister's success really diminish her? Is their relationship a zero sum game where only so much success has been granted to the entire family and her older sister has greedily usurped it? Or is it her fault for taking everything so personally and seeing everything that happens in terms of a contest with her sister?

The Shield of Blame

If it is the younger sister's fault for personalizing events and seeing everything that happens as a contest with her older sister, is she then not responsible for her recurring wounds and her ongoing anguish? By habitually blaming her older sister, she has shielded herself from facing her own demons and has failed to take responsibility for improving her life.

The irony she cannot bear to see is that as long as she hides behind her shield of blame, the hidden demons of her nature will continue to possess her. In deflecting her conscious attention from confronting these demons, she has ceded to them the power to shape her life as they see fit. In effect, by not taking responsibility for her dilemma she has abandoned herself to the most destructive aspects in her nature. As long as she continues to abandon herself by failing to take responsibility for her predicament, her jealousy and hatred will continue to diminish her and destroy her life. This is where taking things personally takes us in the end.

The Path of Most Resistance

As long as the younger sister insists on taking things personally and viewing everything from the perspective of conflict with her older sister, the darkness and jealousy within her nature will not be challenged. The negative emotional blocks in both her body and soul cannot be cleared; her will remains broken, and her life will be unchanged. By taking things personally, she has chosen the path of most resistance, a path on which she will struggle mightily against her better self, pitting her basest instincts against her true potential. The path of most resistance leads to a life of increased suffering. This is the life path she has chosen for herself, although she lacks the clarity to see that she has chosen it. How could anyone be so foolish? Yet people choose the path of most resistance all the time.

Moving Down

Because the younger sister sees the older sister as the source of her pain, the only direction in which her life can move is down. She has cast herself in the role of the chronic victim, and she can only deteriorate from there. Her agony will grow. Her rage will consume her. The loudest voices in her head will be those of bitterness and hatred. They will make her hard, defensive, and aloof. They will impel her to shun the company of positive people and lead her to feel alone, unappreciated, and misunderstood. She will wallow in self-pity and depression. Unfortunately, she will not sink in her toxicity alone, but in the manner of a stealth virus, she will contaminate those who are emotionally dependent upon her. Her toxicity will certainly affect her son, drawing him toward an even deeper darkness than the one in which he is now immersed.

The tragedy of the younger sister's story is that none of this need happen. The path of most resistance is not an absolute, unchangeable reality. It can be easily avoided. If the younger sister had chosen the path of responsibility and faced her own darkness rather than continuing on her stubborn, lonely walk down the twisted path of most resistance, a better reality would have been able to manifest in her life. Had she transformed herself, the conflict that she created and sustained with her older sister would no longer exist. Instead of chronic tension between them, there would be support for each other. They would be able to applaud each other's successes, and in all likelihood, her son would be better adjusted, perhaps as successful in his life as his cousins have been in their lives. Her reward would be group consciousness, cohesion, and love within the family, rather than jealousy, animosity, and conflict. The family would be an open system with no ceiling on the success its individual members might attain, instead of a closed system, where success is limited and the individual members have to fight each other for their quota of success.

Zero Sum Games

When we *personalize* our experience as the younger sister has, we see ourselves as victims. As victims, we struggle to assert ourselves against our adversary. This forces us to play a zero sum game, struggling to take back our power from those we feel have stolen it. The more we react, the more separation we create between ourselves and those we view as our antagonists. That external separation is also mirrored internally, as increased distance between our ego and our soul. If we are not careful, both the internal and external degrees of separation may prove impossible to surmount. Even if we should win the zero sum game, we would still lose in the long term because we are not advancing our growth, only strengthening our negativity and the power it has over us. This is the opposite of living a responsible and conscious life.

Whenever we take things personally, we create a closed system and lock ourselves into a zero sum game. Zero sum games are not limited to individuals, but also apply to competing interest groups. Wherever and whenever people organize their lives and perceptions of reality around their toxicity, zero sum games will always be played.

The Cycle of Personalization

Zero sum games are the end product of the cycle of personalization. This cycle has three phases:

↦ *We take things personally.*

↦ *We create a closed system where it's us versus them.*

↦ *We are forced by our own foolishness into playing a zero sum game.*

A more intelligent and conscious response would be to avoid the inevitable struggle for power that occurs when we personalize events and to turn inward instead to face the toxic energies in our system that need clearing. When we clear our subconscious of its toxicity, we won't be as likely to fall back into the instinctive reactive patterns and the closed system that first wounded and then weakened us. We will also have enough strength and lucidity to avoid the traps others may set for us in the hope that we will react to their ploys, and allow them to hurt us.

A Lost Opportunity

What the younger sister failed to realize in creating her closed system is that when we turn another person into a scapegoat, we lose an opportunity to advance our growth and evolution. If we are too scared to face ourselves, we are too scared to grow. If we refuse to face our false self, we will not find our true self. Jealousy and envy are always self-destructive. When someone is jealous, they can never be satisfied, content, or find peace. Their moments of vengeance only provide them with temporary relief. When a person's system is toxic, nothing brings them peace.

The Relative Nature of Personalizing Reality

Taking things personally, then, is always dangerous to our well-being. *We take things personally when we view the world relatively, not as it is, but as it affects our own sense of self.* If we permit another person to negatively impact our self-worth, we will react to that encroachment very personally. We will become hostile and angry, wishing to hurt them as much as, or more than they hurt us. When we react personally, we start a fresh cycle of internal violence in our lives. That violence might never be translated into action, but it will color our thoughts and influence our feelings. It will increase our stress, release toxic chemicals into our bloodstream, and destroy our peace. When we react personally, we lose our objectivity and clarity. We are no longer detached. Our soul connection is severed. We are more interested in retaliation and vindication than in growth and evolution.

The Healthy Ego and Group Consciousness

When we develop a healthy ego, taking things personally, creating a closed system, and playing zero sum games no longer interests us. We now know better. If there's enough success in the world for you, then there's also enough for me. Even better, if I am whole and successful, it will be easier for you to be whole and successful. The more wholeness and abundance we both generate, the easier it will be for everyone else to find abundance.

When we view reality through the lens of *I win/you win*, reality expands. A win/win model generates communication, cooperation, and teamwork - all elements of group consciousness. Whenever group consciousness exists, peace and order flourish, and economic opportunity expands. For a healthy sense of group consciousness to flourish, everyone who participates in the group must have cleared the toxicity from their system. Otherwise the group consciousness will be shallow, false, and short lived. Instead of leading to peace, it will lead to blame, bitterness, and cynicism.

Zero Sum Reality

When we view reality through the traditional lens of *I win/you lose*, reality contracts. There is no group consciousness. Life is war, a series of zero sum games. The traditional win/lose model engenders conflict, misunderstanding, and instability. All we have to do is look at the world of today to realize how entrenched we are in this model of reality.

We can never transform our consciousness or begin to change the world until we address the hidden, negative elements in our own system. Every attempt at transformation and change that fails to address our toxicity will fail to meet its objective.

Refusing to Take Things Personally

The good news is that when we refuse to take things personally, we won't have to react. Reacting negatively is a choice, not an inevitable occurrence. We react negatively when we feel powerless. That is the lesson Barbara learned when she cleared her toxicity and healed her childhood wounds. Once she realized that she didn't have to suppress her own needs in order to be loved, she found that standing up for her self was empowering and exhilarating. When she stood up for herself, she stood in her own power and her self-pity vanished. Rather than feeling less than everyone else, she recognized herself as the equal of everyone she encountered.

Reationships and Group Consciousness

In establishing positive and constructive relationships with other people, a person with a healthy ego is beginning to stretch his self-concept and open himself up to becoming a channel of unconditional love. When a group of people with healthy egos gets together, unconditional love is present and palpable. Love is the basis of equality. When unconditional love is present, everyone in the group feels both unique *and* equal. When unconditional love is absent, people struggle against each other to stand out and be unique. What is natural and obvious when our eyes are open with love is no longer accessible or apparent once love's clarity is lost. When love dissolves, group consciousness no longer exists.

To illustrate these ideas, lets imagine a large, multi-generational family. The parents have several children. These children are now all grown up, married with teenage children of their own. One young teenager dislikes one of his cousins and has for a long time but keeps his animosity hidden. The only hint of his disdain is that he is cool to his cousin.

One Sunday, there is a family gathering at the grandparents' home. Some of the boys decide to play touch football in the backyard. The boy who is secretly disliked by his cousin lines up as a receiver on offense and goes out for a pass. The cousin who detests him is the defensive back on the other team. The play develops. The receiver runs his route. He breaks open for a moment. The ball is thrown, a perfect strike. He turns to make the catch. Instead of trying to break up the play, the defender goes for his cousin, hitting him with a vicious shot in the back of his thighs. The boy flies up in the air then falls on the base of his spine in pain and shock. After all, this is touch football, not tackle, and tackling is not allowed. The receiver gets slowly to his feet and confronts his cousin. This, of course, is just what the resentful cousin hoped would happen. He wants his unsuspecting cousin to start something so he will have the excuse he needs to hit him with the full fury of his resentment. Words are spoken in anger. Insults are hurled back and forth. Pushing ensues. The receiver takes a wild swing at his cousin and misses.

The cousin who has set up the entire situation is a stone cipher. No emotion breaks through the cold mask of his face, his hard eyes the only hint of the hatred that lies beneath. In his head where no one can see his thoughts, he secretly exults. You've just made your fatal mistake cousin, he says silently to himself. You did just what I wanted you to do. You've given me the green light to destroy you. A hint of a smile plays at the ends of his lips. His right arm moves forward suddenly in a quick, compact motion. He hits his cousin as hard as he can in the face. The boy collapses, his lip split, his face bloodied.

Pandemonium breaks out. The other boys go running into the house. The adults quickly come running out. The father of the boy who has been hit confronts his nephew. His younger brother, the father of the resentful cousin comes to his son's defense. Pretty soon the two brothers are pushing each other, giving new life to old grudges from their own teenage years. The other brothers and sisters try to break up the widening dispute to no avail. Instead of ending the conflict, they are drawn into it.

The conflict has now escalated to a new level, moving through the generations and splitting the family into factions. The long-term cohesiveness of the family has been ruined. The entire family is now highly reactive and out of control. Each faction is self-righteous, certain the other side is wrong. Each faction wants to dominate and punish the other one. Even the grandparents are on different sides of the family conflict. In the blink of an eye the family has shifted from group consciousness to zero sum warfare. Instead of allowing love and respect to hold the family together, they are now all fighting for domination and control. Everybody wants to be right. The situation has become highly polarizing. The negative energy they have foolishly and unconsciously created together now has a life of its own and will draw them further apart. In the end, the conflict will wound and diminish everybody. There will be no winners.

Was any of this really necessary? One person, infected with a smoldering resentment, contaminated the entire family, reawakened forgotten tensions, and created group conflict. A once loving family with a long history of cohesion reacted to conflict with more conflict and lost its cohesive center in the blink of an eye.

As our example suggests, it is easy to lose love, easy to react, and easy to create conflict with little provocation. While the above example is imaginary, it is not far-fetched. Things like this happen all the time and are but a reminder of the covert and insidious nature of evil. If we are easily provoked and allow ourselves to react inappropriately, we open the door to evil and thoughtlessly invite it into our lives.

If the cousin who had been tackled had recognized the resentment in his cousin's actions and been able to maintain his self-control, he might have gotten up, walked away, and said nothing. Instead, he reacted and helped his cousin hurt him. Instead of walking away from trouble, he walked into trouble, and the rest of the family followed suit. This is one of those times when it would have been far better to turn the other cheek than to let one's ego get in the way. It takes a clear and mature person to have the wisdom and self-control to recognize when it is time to walk away from trouble. While it is no easy task, neither is it an impossible one.

The Times We Live In

We live in an age of increasing polarity and deepening conflict in all spheres of human experience: between nations, religions, political ideologies, ethnicities, genders, families, and individuals. This conflict is global, regional, local, political, economic, environmental, cultural, religious, historical, and increasingly personal. Sometimes, it is all of these things at once. Virtually all forms of this conflict involve closed systems and zero sum games. No matter the conflict, there is little honest dialogue between the opposing parties. Instead of dialogue, charges and counter charges are levied, irreconcilable demands are made, and hostilities follow.

With the world driven by the increasing spread of negative energies, the end of conflict frequently appears too late, if at all, and when it does arrive, it is often temporary. Instead of turning over a new leaf and building toward a new future, this becomes a time when new seeds of hatred are planted. The vanquished nurture their wounds and sow their bitterness in deep, underground streams of hatred that lie boiling within their psyches. Inevitably, the conflict returns.

We stand once more at a critical point in world history. We live in a time of great uncertainty. The storm winds gather; the chill of peril fills the air. As dark as the times may be, not all is lost. We still stand. While the gathering storm may bring us into harms way, it also presents us with an unparalleled opportunity for personal growth and spiritual advancement. If we choose the path of personal evolution, we will increase the light in this world and lessen the power of the darkness to wreak havoc all around us. The most important thing we can do for the world is to be who we really are.

The future is on our shoulders. At a time when, as individuals, we may seem to be insignificant, the truth is that we have never been more powerful. We have never been more important, and we have never been more necessary. If we succeed in bringing down the light from above, our influence will expand in ways we may never know about and touch people in other parts of the world whom we never knew existed.

ten ELEVATION

*The problems that exist in the world today cannot be
solved by the level of thinking that created them.*

Albert Einstein

*It is high time that the ideal of success should be
replaced by the ideal of service.*

Albert Einstein

*The weak can never forgive. Forgiveness is the attribute
of the strong.*

Mahatma Gandhi

In the Elimination and Integration Zones of the transformational
journey, there are two essential tasks in each zone that must be completed if we hope to succeed when we reach the Elevation Zone. In the
Elimination Zone, we must clear our system of its toxicity then open the
door to the soul. When we complete these two tasks, we become more
whole and integrated. The negative will no longer drag us down, while
the positive and inspiring energies of the soul will be well positioned
to lift us up.

In the Integration Zone, we must stabilize our system and learn to
stand in our power. To accomplish the first task, we must set effective
boundaries to protect our core self from being exploited. To fulfill the
second task, we must reach out to others, help build group consciousness by contributing to the civic good, and become a channel for unconditional love. Once we are clear, whole, and centered, we have established
the necessary foundation to elevate our lives.

Fusion

The expansion of our conscious power marks the beginning of the Elevation Zone. One of the critical tasks of the Elevation Zone is the fusion of the soul and the ego. This fusion creates a direct channel for the wisdom, unconditional love, creativity, and healing energies of the soul to flow into the conscious mind. The synthesis of the formerly disparate elements of consciousness that occurs in the act of fusion connects the two poles of our being, uniting substance with spirit and creating a bridge across which the Divine light can flow quietly into this world.

Fusion and the Ego

When this fusion occurs, the ego is transformed once again. It is no longer simply the healthy ego, learning to stand in its own power, expanding its sense of self in positive and supportive relationships, and beginning to grasp the significance and power of unconditional love. It is now the surrendered ego, the agent of the soul, and the voice of illumination, understanding, and compassion. The surrendered ego's mission is to increase the power of the soul in the life of the individual and to manifest the individual's true identity and purpose. Gandhi, Einstein, Mother Teresa, the Dalai Lama, and Nelson Mandela are all examples of individuals who successfully fused their soul and personality in modern times.

By the time we reach the Elevation Zone, the covert whispers of the negative ego and its dangerous liaison with our toxicity is long over. Where the ego was once the command and control center for the worst elements in our nature, it is now the channel for the highest and most redemptive aspects of our character. As we heal and transform the ego, we redeem our lives.

In its base phase, the ego's orientation is negative. It is an agent of separation, dominated by fear, and has no interest in the growth or evolution of the individual. Control and power dominate its agenda.

In its middle phase, the ego's orientation is positive and healthy. It is striving to escape the shadow of fear that has dominated the individual and to overcome habitual behaviors and reactive patterns that have reinforced the power of the negative in the life of its host. The healthy ego is a vehicle of integration. It is learning to love unconditionally and stand in the power of the soul.

In its highest phase, the ego is neither positive nor negative, but has surrendered to the soul and become detached from desire. The surrendered ego is emotionally balanced and centered in the light. It shines with inner peace and is radiant with joy. Unlike the negative ego, the surrendered ego is clear of hopeless entanglements and negative consequences. The surrendered ego is the Divine's ambassador in this world.

Karma and Freedom

Not surprisingly, the only significant contribution the negative ego makes that will endure beyond the death of the body is the negative karma it created while it held power. Its legacy is more toxicity that will have to be processed and cleared in other lifetimes. In the time that it is here, the negative ego finds few answers to life and experiences precious little fulfillment. Instead, it tarnishes the soul with its intrigues, contributes to its burdens, causes it to lose its momentum toward the light, and adds to its karmic weight.

The surrendered ego does just the opposite. It is focused on freedom, knowing that freedom is found only when we move in harmony with the Divine. It realizes that freedom is never strictly an individual or separate phenomenon, but is the result of a union between the individual, his soul, and the Divine. Until the Divine confers its light and power upon us, our experience of our true identity and purpose remains limited to our orientation in time and space, and we will be unable to experience the timeless dimension of our nature. We simply cannot know who we really are when we are only aware of part of ourselves. Without the presence of the Divine in our system, our true identity remains unknown, and we remain unfulfilled.

The Process of Self-Realization

The first major step in the process of Self-realization occurs with the fusion of our ego and our soul. That merger transpires in the Elevation

Zone and must occur before the final illumination of our identity can take place. When the two poles of our nature merge, final union with the Divine usually follows in short order. When that merger does occur, our soul becomes infinitely brighter. With the Divine light pouring through our consciousness, we will experience a sense of universality and oneness with all life. Our deepest identity springs from our sense of universality. We are not one thing or one person, separated from the rest of the world by our skin and our ego. We are a part of everything. Our essence is the essence of all things, and the essence of all things is also our essence. We are neither separate nor alone. We are all one in our own selves yet also part of a continuous organic whole that pulsates with life, light, and energy. We are no more and no less than anyone else. We are equal to every living thing, and every living thing is equal to us. We have discovered that our real identity is not found in our form, our substance, or our body, for every form and every substance is separate and different from every other form and every other substance. At this juncture we come to understand that our essence and true identity are both found in the light at the core of our being. That light is deathless, formless, and without substance. It is our personal link to the Divine.

❡ Until the time when we merge our soul and ego in the Elevation Zone, that light at the core of our being is but a flicker, but when that merger occurs, our inner light ignites and fans quickly into a bright flame. If we maintain the intensity of that inner flame, we will draw the Divine down to us and experience Self-realization. In that moment, we will know who we really are and what our purpose in the manifested world is to be.

When the Old Order Crumbles

Before reaching the final transformation where it merges with the soul, the surrendered ego has already been through two prior transformational cycles. In clearing the toxicity it once contained, the negative ego died and became lighter.

In standing up to the many challenges to its integrity, the healthy ego became strong, stable, sure of itself, and capable of containing more inner light. In letting go of attachment and desire, the surrendered ego became brighter, more conscious and powerful. As the surrendered ego quickens in the light and pulls down the Divine power to complete its quickening, it becomes one with the underlying unity of all life and realizes its true identity.

The death of the negative ego, and the opening up of the path of light are major acts of grace in the life of the individual. They change everything. Through their auspices the individual undergoes an internal revolution in which the forces of inner darkness are overcome, the ceiling of growth is raised, and the path of personal evolution becomes accessible.

Fusion and the Path

When the surrendered ego fuses with the soul, it becomes the path itself. When the Divine power is consciously present in one's system, there is no separation between path and person. One becomes the path. Instead of seeking the way like the healthy ego does, the surrendered ego becomes the way, and as long as the surrendered ego stays true to the Divine power, it will never lose its way. Its mission is to continue to aspire upward, to reach for ever widening levels of light, and to radiate unconditional love on earth. The surrendered ego knows that the more it gives of itself, the more it will become.

While the surrendered ego knows who it really is and what its purpose is, it also knows that there is no ultimate arrival, no final end to the journey, no absolute realization, just the dynamic progression of consciousness with each state of inner light eventually yielding to a succeeding stage of greater insight. The surrendered ego is totally focused on being one with the light and becoming ever lighter.

Acceptance

The great secret of the surrendered ego is acceptance. It knows that the more it loves unconditionally, the easier it will be to accept whatever situations may come its way. Being in a state of acceptance allows the surrendered ego to remain emotionally centered and connected to the timeless dimension of its nature. As long as the surrendered ego stays in acceptance, it will maintain its connection to the Divine, and the power of the negative will not be able to distract it from its path.

❧ The surrendered ego further recognizes that when it is in acceptance mode it is both a channel for unconditional love to enter the world and a vehicle for prayers to flow up to the Divine world. Whether Divine energy flows down through the open door of the surrendered ego or prayers flow up through it, the result is the same. Good things happen. We all win when Divine power is brought to bear in the world.

The Intersection of Humanity and Divinity

The surrendered ego stands, then, at the intersection of humanity and divinity, knowing that it has a dual role to play. One role is to keep the door between these two realms open. To do this it must maintain its integrity and openness, remaining centered and in acceptance, rather than being pulled in conflicting directions by waves of negative emotion. It cannot afford to take things personally and fall into reactive behavior. Its job is not to get even or yield to the seductive pull of retaliation. Instead, its task is to forgive all transgressions against its person, so that it might remain centered and connected to the Divine. Its high mission is to bring peace, clarity, and balance, wherever, and whenever, it can.

The other role the surrendered ego plays is that of teacher and example, leading the way for others to find the door to the Divine within themselves. It is not interested, as is the negative ego, in being the only power on the playing field. Instead, the surrendered ego wants everyone to share equally in the Divine power, for that is our true birthright.

The surrendered ego knows that once we have discovered who we really are, the most effective way to deepen and expand our experience of our true self is to help other people discover their real self. The surrendered ego knows that we expand our joy when we share our joy.

The Negative Ego and Free Will

In contrast to the surrendered ego, the negative ego does not have the power to grow or move forward. It has no capacity for sustained joy or any connection to the soul. The negative ego's range of emotion proceeds from fear, which is its negative pole, to aggression, which is its positive pole. Most of the negative ego's existence is spent in generating experiences that slide back and forth between these two poles of determination.

The free will of the negative ego, therefore, is bound and limited by the two forces of fear and aggression. While the negative ego may think it has free will, the truth is quite different. Its freedom is severely restricted. There just isn't much room to find peace and freedom between fear and aggression.

We must not forget that the negative ego's mission is to protect the toxicity in our system from being discovered. It sustains its own existence by doing so. When the negative ego succeeds in deterring us from facing our toxicity it insures that our suffering will be continual and chronic. By placing its need to dominate ahead of our need to grow, the negative ego prevents us from becoming more conscious.

The Relative Nature of Identity

Without conscious access to our soul, all perceptions and conceptions of our identity are relative and changeable. Our perceptions of identity are related to the roles we play in life, rather than to the core self that stands behind those roles. The difference between one's role, and one's core self can best be understood by observing an accomplished actor working at his craft. A skilled actor is able to submerge his own identity in the roles he plays, but when the show is over and the shooting done, the actor reemerges as the person he really is. His real world and sense of self are very different from the world and role of the character he has left behind.

The difference between the accomplished actor and the rest of us is that while the actor can step out of his character and leave the role he plays behind him, most of us cannot step out of ourselves and put our roles behind us. Our roles define us, and we have great difficulty separating what we do from who we are.

However, when we gain access to our soul and begin to elevate our life, all that starts to change. As we open to unconditional love and stretch our ego toward our soul, our sense of identity begins to shift slowly from what we do to who we are. While what we do is relative and can always change or be taken away from us, who we are is permanent and can never be lost.

The Different Levels of Identity

Obviously, our sense of who we are will be different if we are dominated by the negative ego, opened to the healthy ego, or transformed by the surrendered ego. Each stage of the ego's development will give us a different view of our identity. Those views become more accurate and truer to whom we really are as we move up through the three ego levels. The truest and most satisfying sense of self comes from the surrendered ego. It is the only stage of the ego that has truly merged with the soul and moved beyond the limitations of form and substance.

The least satisfying sense of self comes from the negative ego. It stands completely separate and alone from the soul and has no connection higher than its own fear and arrogance. The negative ego determines its own identity by the role, or roles, it plays, as well as by how much power it can pull its way and place under its thumb.

The negative ego faces a difficult dilemma. If it does what it has been commissioned to do, which is to protect the individual from further pain, it will survive. However, if it survives, its host will never find real and lasting happiness, discover his true nature or actualize his higher purpose. He will remain separate, alone, and bound in fear. The controlling principle of the negative ego is that whatever remains alone and unconnected to a divine source will continue to remain empty and unfulfilled. At the heart of the negative ego is a state of deprivation that no longing or desire can ever fill. The negative ego may acquire many things, gain great power and notoriety, be the envy of many in the world, but it will never flower, as the example of Septimius clearly suggests. Nothing succeeds for the negative ego like its own death, yet the negative ego will fight its dying with all its considerable strength.

When the healthy ego becomes stabilized in the Integration Zone, its compass becomes permanently fixed on true spiritual North, and it is guided by a deepening thirst for union with the soul. It begins to focus acutely on reaching the Elevation Zone. Of course, it knows that as a result of this pursuit, it will eventually die, but unlike the negative ego stage that has just passed, the healthy ego does not fear its demise. Rather it seeks it out instead. Since it has cleared its internal toxicity, it does not fear change, for it knows that the core self not only never dies, but also grows brighter and stronger as we evolve. It knows that its own death is the key to a wider life and to rapprochement with the soul. Its mission is to facilitate that union. It is not an obstruction as the negative ego is, but a dedicated servant of the evolutionary process.

The Surrendered Soul and Identity

The connection with the soul, of course, is the basis of the surrendered ego's identity. Because it is conscious of its Divine connection, the surrendered ego knows that it is both a part of all that is and one with all that is at the same time. The surrendered ego, then, is aware that it is the gate to our multidimensional nature. It encompasses the individual and the universal, the temporal and the eternal, the mortal and the immortal, and the finite and the infinite. It is no longer empty, unhappy, and unfulfilled. It has no further need of desire and is free of desires and compulsions. Armed with its ability to love life and accept whatever happens in life, the surrendered ego is sustained by its conscious connection to the Divine.

Exclusivity and the Divine Condition

The Divine energy is not at all exclusive. It is available to everyone equally. However, in order to receive the energy of the Divine into our system, we must be ready to hold its power, and must be conscious and whole enough to use that power in a responsible and purposeful manner. If we do not meet the Divine's criteria, the Divine power will not merge with us. Paramahansa Yogananda, the great Indian spiritual teacher, put it this way. "When He shall be sure that nothing else will claim you, then He will come." The Divine, after all, created the game of life, and to succeed in life we must play by His rules, not ours. The sooner we understand those rules, the sooner we will be ready to succeed.

⟨ The main rule in the game of life is clear and simple. The Divine is not exclusive. It is merely our lack of consciousness that separates us from the Divine. The only barriers between the Divine and the person we are meant to be are those we ourselves erect.

When we succeed in connecting with the Divine, the higher energy of that connection will change our experience. This represents a quantum leap forward in our consciousness. It raises our energy, sharpens our acuity, deepens our peace, extends our intuition, and reveals our purpose. Union with the Divine also softens our edges and improves our sense of humor.

It may come as a surprise, considering the overly serious and pious nature of most religions, but the Divine is happy and joyful. If more of us took the time to discover who we really were, the world would be a much happier and safer place. The epidemic of imbalance and toxicity that plagues the planet would be over.

The Tools of Elevation

The major tools of the Elevation Zone are straightforward and extremely powerful. They encompass a four-fold approach and include:

- *Service*
- *Meditation*
- *Prayer*
- *Integration and Activation of the Will*

Service

We serve others in order to grow our soul, increase our inner light, and fuse our soul with our ego. However, if we try to serve before we have cleared our toxicity, opened our system to our soul, and learned to stand in our power, our service will not be empowering. Instead, it will be draining and sacrificial.

Service elevates us when we have established soul contact and our system is open and clear enough to pull down the light from above. When those two factors are in place, the Divine will give the energy that we give to others back to us in greater quantity and higher quality. When we choose to serve others, God chooses to serve us. As we work to lift others up, God works to lift us up. Service upgrades the quality of the energy circulating in our system, and that upgraded energy draws us ever closer to our soul and spirit.

The X Factor

The unknown, or X factor in the equation of service is our conscious intent. Is that intent selfless, or is it selfish and manipulative? If our service has a selfish motive and our intention is to promote ourselves instead of helping others, then that "service" won't promote our growth, elevate our consciousness, or release spiritual energy into the world. Because we're using and not giving, the inner door won't open, and Divine energy won't flow down to us. The secret to divine intervention is to give from the heart without expectation or selfish motive. In true service, there is no quid pro quo.

Selfishness and Service

Selfishness is the product of one's separation from his soul. The separate self has no connection to anything greater and more encompassing than itself. It sees itself as alone in a hostile world. It has no real capacity for love. If it gives, it will only do so to make it easier to get what it wants. It only serves to make itself look good. It is not interested in doing good works. It is ruled by fear, greed, and desire and will pursue its own agenda relentlessly.

The negative ego cannot comprehend the motives of those who have been drawn to serve others and is suspicious of those who do. Its only interest is its self-interest. It cannot conceive of altruism nor consider any action in which it will receive less than it gives. It does not know what the healthy ego is learning or what the surrendered ego has mastered. Through service, we contribute to the well-being of other people, and in so doing, we consolidate our relationship to our soul and deepen our own sense of unity.

While service may be used by the negative ego to achieve its agenda, it is essentially a technique for transforming the healthy ego into the surrendered ego. By serving others unselfishly we pull down the Divine energies into our lives. It is the Divine energy working within our system that eventually fuses our soul with our ego. When that fusion takes place, the healthy ego dies, and the surrendered ego is born.

Those we serve may not reward us for our good deeds or even acknowledge them, but that is not the point. By serving others, we serve our highest interests, open our psyches wider to the Divine light, and quicken our growth. Inner growth is the whole point of service and is its real reward.

Service and The Present Moment

When our service is clean, we connect with other people in a deep way. That connection creates a sense of unity and purpose that shifts us out of self-concern and into the present moment, where anxiety, need, and attachment do not exist. When we set our own concerns aside, we create the present moment.

We experience the present moment when we are integrated and the two poles of our nature, soul and substance, are in balance. When we are in the present moment, we feel whole and fulfilled, creative, energetic, and alive. The present moment is a psychological state. It always exists, but it disappears when we are preoccupied with self-concern, worry and stress. If we don't find the present moment we won't find our true identity.

Service as an Investment in Our Future

While service is a key to the present moment and to discovering our true identity, it is also an investment in our future. Service creates positive momentum in our life, our contributions to others becoming *credits* in our "spiritual bank account." Those credits mean that life will reward us for our good works at a moment of its choosing and in a time when we might need it most.

The principle behind the idea of a "spiritual bank account" is that when we put out positive energy into the world in the form of good works, we will draw good energy back to us when we need it most. According to the Law of Consequences like attracts like. Negative karma will draw negative conditions and experiences to us. Conversely, positive karma will draw positive and uplifting experiences to us.

Karmic Actions

Negative karma guarantees that we will not evolve further until we resolve the problems our actions have created for us. Negative karma robs our life of positive momentum. The more negative karma in our spiritual bankbook, the less good will that we have to draw from, and the less protected we will be in the future. When we need help, there will be no help. Life will not support us because we supported no one unless it served our own selfish agenda. Despite the fact that Richard Nixon occupied the most powerful office in the world, that office could not protect him from his karma.

Three Important Principles of Karma

Richard Nixon's fall from grace reveals three important principles of the Law of Consequence. The first principle is that the energy we amass in our spiritual bankbook over our lifetime is more powerful than any position of power we might hold. Nothing will shield us from our karma when the time has come to pay for our actions.

The second principle is that the Law of Consequences is infinitely patient. It manifests when the timing is right for it to produce the necessary effect in the life of the person who created the karma. Its intent is to shock the person who has brought that negative karma on himself into changing his ways. In the process of actualizing an individual's negative karma, the Law of Consequences will often deprive that person of what he desires and values most.

The third principle of the Law of Consequences is implied in the two previous ones. What happens in the invisible world of energy determines what will happen in the manifested world of experience. What we do in the here and now creates a mass of energy that determines what life will later do to us. Nothing happens in a vacuum or without consequences. Our past and present actions are connected to our future experiences. Those causative actions have consequences that will reverberate in our lives long after they have been forgotten.

The only control we can exercise over the future is limited by what we have done in the past and by what we choose to do now. The wise person understands the working of the Law of Consequences and chooses to live his life as constructively as possible. By acting unselfishly with honor, compassion, strength, and integrity, the wise person helps others, contributes to the well-being of the world, and guards the future.

The Fool and the Karmic Highway

The foolish person ignores the correlation between action and consequence. Instead, he proceeds down the karmic highway where most other people, also ignorant of spiritual law, join him. The karmic highway is a perpetual traffic jam, full of angry people jostling for position. No one goes very fast on that highway, but everyone tries to do so nevertheless.

The wise person watches life unfolding on the karmic highway and wonders why so many people are in such a determined rush to go nowhere. They certainly aren't at peace or very happy, yet despite their unhappiness, they refuse to change.

The wise person knows that when we create more negative karma, we generate more schisms between our soul and our ego. These schisms take us farther away from our true nature. The farther we travel from our true nature, the harder it is to return and the longer it will take us to do so.

Since the act of creating negative karma separates us from our true nature, it also destroys our capacity to be in the present moment. As a result, when we choose the way of karma over the path of service, three things happen and none of them are very good. We endanger our connection to our true nature. We lose our coherence with the present moment, and we deplete what credits may still remain in our spiritual bank account. Going down the karmic highway puts at risk everything we may have achieved in the right way.

The Long-term

While karmic acts may initially help us satisfy a selfish agenda and achieve short-term success, in the long-term those same acts will bring us to a far different conclusion. In the end, karmic success dissipates, just as it dissipated for Richard Nixon, and we are left unprotected and exposed with no alternative but to face the long-term consequences of our actions. When the long-term reversal of fortune occurs, an endless nightmare often replaces a relatively short period of prosperity, and a deep depression may displace our former sense of invincibility.

Ultimately, the Law of Consequences forces us to learn a hard lesson. We get away with nothing. There is always a price to pay for creating negative karma, and we never know when, or how, that bill will be presented to us. We control what we do, but we do not control what will happen to us as a result of what we have done. The Law of Consequences always has the last word and in that regard, it is far more powerful than we are. The invisible world of energy and principle rules much of what happens in the visible world. The wise course of action is to serve our highest interests, rather than scheming and plotting in the service of our greed.

Forms of Service

Assuming that we wish to elevate our lives, increase the positive energy in our spiritual account, and do what we can to safeguard our future, what then is the best way to serve?

If we wish to serve and elevate our lives, the first thing we should do is begin at the beginning. We don't have to change our job, enter the priesthood, take a vow of poverty, dedicate our life to helping the poor, or lead a nation to freedom. We don't have to be a saint or a superman.

In fact, we don't have to do, or be, anyone special. We just need to adjust our attitude. The first change we need to make is subtle and simple. We should try to be helpful to those around us, at home, at work, and wherever we go. Remember the golden rule, and do unto others, as we would have them do unto us.

If we do that conscientiously every day, our realm of service will grow because our opening to unconditional love will grow through the service we render. If we give others love and kindness, we eventually become love and kindness. If we accept others for who they are, we begin to accept ourselves for who we really are. The good news about service is this: we become what we give.

As we open to unconditional love through service, we may find ourselves led to serve in other ways. If we listen to our inner self, we will always be led to the form of service that is in harmony with our nature and satisfies our own needs for growth. If it feels right internally in either our heart or our solar plexus, it will be the right thing for us to do. If it feels wrong, if we get a feeling of discomfort or a sense of danger or the distinct impression that we should stay away, then we should. In order to follow our intuitive promptings, it is important to learn to trust our inner feelings.

The Dangers of Service

When we clear our toxicity and open a space for our soul to guide us, our feelings will be one important way that our soul communicates with us. That will not be true, however, if our system is still clogged with toxic content. When toxic content is unresolved, our inner feelings will not represent the one still voice of the soul speaking to us in unambiguous terms. Instead, what we feel will represent the many loud voices of our toxicity.

The other thing we should be aware of when choosing to serve is that we can't be everything to everyone. We do what we can, but we do not do everything that everyone demands of us. Ideally, constructive service should help us discover our identity, but if we give away our core self and all our energy, we will be in danger of destroying our identity and depleting our energy instead. If we let others take advantage of us, control our lives, or steal a piece of our soul, then that is exactly what will happen. To serve constructively, we must be strong, secure in ourselves, and emotionally stable. If we are weak, insecure, and unstable, service will weaken us further. Service is an important part of the elevation process, but it should not be attempted before we have cleared our toxicity, opened the pathway to our soul, and established strong boundaries to protect our core self.

eleven The Nature Of The Will

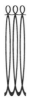

When the solution is simple, God is listening.
Albert Einstein

*The intuitive mind is a sacred gift and the rational
mind is a faithful servant. We have created a society
that honors the servant and has forgotten the gift.*
Albert Einstein

Numerous repercussions accompany our failure to seek our growth. Among the most serious of these consequences is the influence unconscious toxicity has on the will. Unconscious toxicity fragments the will, prevents us from standing in our power, and blocks us from discovering our true identity. As long as the will is fragmented we cannot fuse our mind and soul or increase our inner light. However, when we clear our system of its unconscious toxicity we have created the necessary internal conditions to reintegrate the will, increase our inner light, and stand in our power.

The Physical Will

The will exists in both the physical and the supra-physical domains of our system. The physical will is a product of the conscious mind, the ego, and the emotions. In its operating mode, the physical will is composed of intention, focus, determination, persistence, and perseverance. The physical will attempts to push forward no matter how difficult the challenge or how dire the circumstance. Its purpose is to sustain us in times of adversity and to help us overcome the obstacles we encounter in life. These are important qualities. Tenacity counts.

There is, however, an intrinsic danger to be found in relying too heavily on the physical will. While the physical will is certainly endowed with stubbornness, it is not necessarily endowed with intelligence. It tends to be emotional rather than cool and objective in its manifestation. Since the physical will is rather over-weighted toward inflexibility, it often encourages us to persist in situations that are actually detrimental to our true interest. As long as toxic material resides in our system, those dangers are amplified. A strong negative ego, with an elevated level of repressed anger to sustain it, compounds the inherent stubbornness of the physical will and can influence us to persist in self-destructive behavior.

The Supra-Physical Will

The supra-physical will functions in an entirely different manner. It is a unified and coherent force of superior intelligence and clarity whose main purpose is to elevate our lives. When it is activated, it accelerates our growth and evolution. It is a flexible instrument rather than a stubborn one and, as a rule, will not lead us into harm's way or down a path of self-destruction. However, it will not flinch from confrontation and adversity if conflict is necessary to its purpose. Sometimes, self-sacrifice is the only way as it was in the life of Christ. Thankfully, however, self-sacrifice is the exception, not the rule.

The supra-physical will is composed of spiritual light, not emotion and ego. It is highly intelligent and linked to a higher source of wisdom and power beyond the rational mind. As a result of that link, it sees further into the future than the conscious mind ever can. As long as toxicity is present in one's system, that toxicity separates the physical will from the supra-physical will. That separation fractures the will and prevents its integration. The result of a fractured will is that growth is checkmated and psychic energy is dissipated through internal struggle.

The Fractured Will

A fractured will is like a raucous political party with many competing factions holding its nominating convention for national office. During the convention, every faction competes with every other faction, hoping that it is their agenda, and not that of their competitor's, that will be adopted by the party's platform. Unlike a political party, however, the moment of definitive triumph never arrives for the fractured will. Rather than accomplishing a final resolution of competing positions and uniting behind a candidate and a platform, the struggle for supremacy within the will remains constant and unremitting. The unrelenting nature of that struggle makes it very difficult, if not impossible, to elevate our life.

The internal struggle for supremacy of the will involves the three major domains of our nature: the spiritual, the conscious, and the subconscious. As long as this struggle persists, the domain that is the most negative will be the most dominant.

Since the will of the spirit is always positive, it has no way of achieving dominance when the will is in a fractured state. When the will is fractured, the spiritual will is forced to the sidelines, relegated to being a bystander and not a participant in our life. As long as toxic elements remain in the subconscious, the will of the subconscious is the default domain of the will. The governing beliefs that reside there will determine much of what occurs in our life.

While toxic elements persist in the subconscious, the will of the subconscious is both deterministic and adversarial. It is deterministic in that the toxic and shaming experiences previously stored in the subconscious will draw people and events into our life that mirror those toxic patterns. It is adversarial because while those toxic elements persist in the subconscious, the will of the subconscious opposes both the conscious and the spiritual will.

If the conscious will attempts to resist the will of the subconscious and implement its own goals, it not only will fail but also create more internal conflict that further dissipates one's energy. On the other hand, if the conscious will concedes its power to the will of the subconscious, it will be participating in its own undoing. Whenever the will is in a state of fragmentation, the position of the conscious will is untenable, the spiritual will is banished to the sidelines, and the toxic will of the subconscious controls our life.

Separation in the Will

Unresolved toxicity then, fractures the will, circumscribes the power of the conscious will, and eviscerates the power of the spiritual will. A fractured will means we are no longer guided toward fulfillment from above. We no longer have a higher truth or a bright inner light to guide us. We are lost in life without higher protection or true direction.

When we clear our toxicity, however, the will begins to heal and re-formulate itself. When the will is fractured it is controlled by the toxic will of the subconscious, but when the will is unified it is led by its highest component, the spiritual will.

In essence, a fractured will leads to two unsatisfactory results. It prevents us from becoming who we should be, and it manifests what we *don't* want to happen in our life. A unified will, on the other hand, helps us become who we were always meant to be and manifest what we do want in our lives.

The Key to Unifying the Will

Whenever the will is fractured, its three main factions each have a different agenda. The conscious will of the individual wants to move forward and find happiness in what it desires for itself. The spiritual will wants the individual to enter the path of personal evolution and elevate his life, while the will of the subconscious wants the individual to repeat the past, maintain the status quo, and remain in pain, confusion, and unhappiness.

The key to unifying the will, like almost everything else, lies in the transformation of our toxicity. The governing beliefs stored in the subconscious run counter to what we might consciously want to have happen in our life. These controlling beliefs cannot be accessed or controlled by our conscious mind. Therefore, as long as these beliefs persist, they will continue to subvert and fracture our will. These unconscious beliefs give the subconscious a mind of its own with a set of purposes that are unique to it. We might not consciously understand what those purposes are, or that they even exist, but they control our lives nevertheless.

Each governing belief seeks to pull the subconscious in a different direction. This means the will is not only fractured by unconscious toxic material into spiritual, conscious, and subconscious components, but it also means that the will of the subconscious may itself be fragmented into further factions.

The only aspect of our self that benefits from the fracturing of the will is the negative ego. Whatever benefits the negative ego, however, is detrimental to our evolution. As long as the will is fractured, the negative ego remains in power, and there will be no end to inner conflict.

The Unified Will

Given the substantial limitations of the fractured will, it is a great advantage in life to have a unified will. The unified will is a coherent and organized force that supports the true purpose and aspirations of the individual. It is focused with all of its elements and all of its considerable power working in concert toward the goal of Self-realization. Its roots lie deep within a clear subconscious. Its trunk flows along the spinal column, and its branches reach high into the mind and soul. It is a real and organic element of consciousness that nurtures and supports the growth of the individual.

In the unified will, the will of the subconscious is no longer negative and uncontrollable. A clear subconscious is easily aligned with the goals of the soul and spirit. There is no more conscious toxicity left to bend the will and break it into pieces. When the will is united and made operational, it connects the physical aspects of our system with our supra-physical ones. The subconscious and conscious elements of the will are reunited with the soul and spirit. As the will is unified, it becomes an elevating force in our life.

The Differentiating Factor

What differentiates someone with a fractured will from someone with a unified will is the amount of unconscious toxicity that resides in his system. The lawyer from chapter six had a shaming father who ridiculed her and wounded her terribly as a young child. Those wounds were toxic to her well-being. As an adult, the trauma she sustained in childhood and buried in her subconscious overruled her conscious attempts to find happiness. She married a man, who shamed and ridiculed her just as her father had done, adding new layers of psychic wounding to her original ones.

The compounding of her original wounds created a new voice in her, one filled with rage, hatred, and hurt. That voice was out of control, vindictive, unstable, and hated all men. The emergence of this voice took her farther from herself than she had ever been before. My client consciously wanted to find happiness as an adult, but her subconscious will had been programmed by her governing beliefs as a child to bring only more shame and ridicule into her life. By bringing more negative experiences into her life, her unconscious toxicity further fractured her subconscious will.

Where the Path Begins

The covert goal of the fractured will is to deprive us of our fulfillment, happiness, and true identity. In addition to bringing what we don't want into our lives, a fractured will cuts us off from our soul. When we are cut off from our soul, we feel alone, unworthy and powerless, and what we then attract into our lives will amplify those feelings. We can have no power over a fractured will until we confront the origins of our toxicity. When we confront our toxicity, the most recent version of our original trauma opens the door to rooting out our unconscious governing beliefs.

In the case of the attorney, her divorce from her husband provided the entry point to clearing her childhood trauma with her father. That entry point is where her path to wholeness began. Like the attorney, we all have an entry point to the path of personal evolution that is unique to our experience.

Denial

When we bury our toxicity in some far corner of our body, we have fled as far as we possibly can from facing it. Despite our best efforts to conceal our pain from our awareness, running away from that pain will not break the link between our toxicity and our life. It will only promote the delusion that we have done so. No matter where we go, or how far we run, the concealed toxicity in our system travels with us, just as it traveled out to sea with Frank and dominated his life for forty years.

What we deny we empower. In formulating our denial, we forget the cardinal law of all denial. What we disown owns us. We can try to walk away from our nature, but our nature will not walk away from us. As long as toxic content remains submerged in our system, it will always be stronger than we are, and its effects on our lives will be devastating. It will break our will, drain our energy, prevent us from elevating our lives, and condemn us to repeating a past we would rather leave behind.

The Intuition and the Body of Light

Unlike the fractured will, which speaks in the many confusing voices of the shame-based personality, the unified will speaks with the one clear voice of the intuition. The intuition is the psyche's higher guide. Its purpose is twofold: to protect us and lead us to fulfillment. It is the North Star of the psyche. If we learn to listen to its quiet voice, we will be guided toward where we must go, and away from where we should not go. We will stay centered and on our path.

When the will is unified, the body is full of inner light, but when the will is broken the body contains more darkness than light. While the broken will is formed by the stagnant energy of toxic shame, the unified will is created by clarity and the dynamic flow of spiritual light. Toxic shame will not take us where we need to go, but the spiritual light of the unified will can take us as far as we are prepared to go.

The fractured will is the agent of fate and leads to ongoing emotional suffering. The unified will is the agent of destiny. It leads to fulfillment. When the will is whole, no more hidden inner barriers remain to prevent us from elevating our lives and realizing who we really are. Self-realization depends on a psyche that is whole and a will that is unified.

The Will as a Living Entity

The supra-physical will is more than an abstract assumption and larger in scope than our conscious determination, intention, and persistence. It is a living entity and must be nourished in order to be effective. We nourish the supra-physical will when we build up the spiritual energy in our system and pull down unconditional love from above. We do this when we clear our toxicity, stand up for ourselves, meditate, pray, and serve others. However, if our will is not already unified, all attempts to nourish it will be in vain. We can't nourish what does not yet exist.

The physical foundation of the supra-physical will is located at the base of the spine. Residing quietly at the base of the spine is a reservoir of spiritual energy that most people are completely unaware of. The ancient spiritual masters of India called this reservoir of energy, Kundalini, the serpent fire. To their clairvoyant sight, this energy resembled a coiled serpent.

The ultimate goal of spiritual practice is to raise the Kundalini energy up the center of the spinal column and into the head. As the Kundalini rises up the spinal column, it increases our inner light. When the Kundalini reaches the forehead, it connects the spiritual center at the base of the spine with the spiritual center in the middle of the forehead. This energy connection unifies the three factions of the will and actualizes the supra-physical will. What was once theory and possibility now becomes tangible reality.

The spiritual center in the middle of the forehead is the third eye of all mystical traditions. In the Gospel of Thomas, Christ referred to this center when he said, " If thine eye be single, thy body will be full of light." When the will is unified and the Kundalini energy flows into the third eye, the body fills with spiritual light. The activation of the supra-physical will ties the spirit and soul to the body and mind. In short, the integration of the will is the basis of all further stages of elevation and Self-realization.

The Seven Spiritual Centers

The third eye is actually the sixth in a series of seven spiritual centers that exist just outside the physical body. The ancient masters of India called these spiritual centers chakras. Chakra is a Sanskrit term that means "a wheel of light." When the chakras fill with Kundalini energy, they expand, become brighter, and spin much more rapidly. As the chakras unfold under the impetus of the Kundalini energy, we begin to awaken to who we really are.

The chakras and the Kundalini energy, which awakens them, are crucial elements of the supra-physical nervous system. They are a vital part of our inner wiring for higher consciousness and spiritual enlightenment. While the Kundalini exists and functions from within the body, the seven chakras are located in the aura or electromagnetic field in front of the body.

The first of the seven major chakras is called the Root Chakra. It is located at the base of the spine, just outside the perineum. It grounds us in our physical body. The Kundalini energy originates from this spiritual center. However, unprocessed toxicity in the hip and pelvic region often blocks this center and prevents the Kundalini from rising. The presence of toxicity in this area keeps the chakras from functioning in anything more than a survivalist mode. Without the Kundalini energy flowing into its appropriate channel, we are like a scrub bush growing in the desert. We can hold on to our position, endure and survive, even thrive in the material world, but we will be prohibited from growing into our true potential.

❧ The second chakra is located just below the navel. The third chakra is located in front of the solar plexus. The fourth chakra is located in front of the center of the chest. The fifth chakra is located in front of the throat. The sixth chakra, of course, is located in front of the center of the forehead. The seventh, or crown chakra is located just above the top of the skull. It is the halo or nimbus frequently painted by medieval artists. We experience Self-realization when the Kundalini energy rises from its source at the base of the spine and flows unimpeded through the middle channel of the central nervous system (the spine) to the top of the head. In order for that higher connection to be made, our system must be clear, integrated, whole, and balanced. When the Kundalini energy connects the base of our spiritual nervous system to the crown chakra at the top of our head, our power is amplified many times. That increase in peak power leads to the realization of our identity and the revelation of our purpose.

The will must be unified before Self-realization can occur. This order of psychic events is indicated by the physiology of the supra-physical system. The spiritual center, which unifies the will, is the sixth chakra, located in the center of the forehead, while the center that confers Self-realization, the seventh chakra, is located above the top of the head. The Kundalini energy enters and activates the supra-physical will before it reaches the crown chakra and awakens us to our true identity.

The Nadis

As the Kundalini energy uncoils and begins its powerful ascent up the central gateway of the spine, it also flows into the secondary energy channels that emanate from the spinal column and travel throughout the body. These secondary channels are called nadis. A complex network of nadis connects the central spinal channel to each of the chakras. As the Kundalini energy travels through the nadi system, it flows into each of the seven chakras in succession, starting from the first chakra at the base of the spine and finishing in the seventh chakra at the top of the head.

As the chakras fill with spiritual light and expand, they open like the petals of a flower and begin to spin very rapidly. The result of releasing the kundalini energy and opening the chakra system is that our body begins to vibrate at a higher rate. The shift in vibratory rate of the energy in the body makes us feel physically lighter, emotionally freer, mentally clearer, and much happier.

The Ego's Surrender

When the Kundalini energy completes its ascent through the chakras, it has completed its essential task of activating the supra-physical nervous system and illuminating our true identity. The activation of the supra-physical nervous system brings the two poles of our nature, body and spirit, into balance.

The union of the physical and supra-physical elements of the nervous system is the basis of the ego's final surrender. With the ego's final sur-render, more spiritual light floods into the mind and body. As more spir-itual light illuminates our system, that light draws our body and mind closer to our soul and spirit. This rapprochement makes it easier for our soul to more accurately imprint our mind with its knowledge and guide it in making the critical choices that will further our growth.

The Two Deaths of the Ego

With each death of the ego our life elevates, our experience of who we are increases, and our opportunities expand. The first death of the ego occurs in the Elimination Zone. This ego death results in the birth of the healthy ego and signals our progression from the Elimination Zone to the Integration Zone.

The second death of the ego signals our movement from the Integration Zone to the Elevation Zone. When the healthy ego dies, the surrendered ego is born. The surrendered ego cannot be born until we activate the supra-physical nervous system and allow it to flood our conscious mind with spiritual light. Without a substantial increase in our spiritual light the healthy ego cannot die. We can't will that death or work within the arena of our thoughts and beliefs to bring it about. The second death of the ego happens when our light is bright enough and our compassion deep enough.

In many ways, the second death of the ego is harder to attain than is the first one. The first death of the negative ego has one central re-quirement. We must clear our toxicity. The second death of the healthy ego has two key requirements. We must increase our light and expand our ability to love unconditionally. The second requirement of learning to love unconditionally suggests that our emotional nature must ripen and mature before the healthy ego finally dies.

Loving unconditionally allows us to be more accepting of life. Learning to love unconditionally is often a struggle. It means we must push ourselves beyond our normal emotional limits and learn to love that which we may find personally abhorrent. However, that does not mean we have to like, or approve of, what we love. Gandhi never stopped loving his opponents, even if he personally disliked them. On the cross, Christ prayed for his executioners. "Forgive them Father," he whispered, "for they know not what they do."

The Two Purposes of Unconditional Love

When we love unconditionally, we are in harmony with our soul. When we react angrily or fearfully, we lose that harmony. Unconditional love has two major purposes. First, it expands our inner harmony and clarifies our sense of purpose. Instead of threatening to start a war of reprisal when events go against us, we will be peaceful and able to formulate a clear, appropriate, and positive response. We won't react and create negative karma. Second, when unconditional love flows through us, it brings emotional healing to the world around us. When we serve our highest needs, we serve the higher needs of others.

My mother, for example, had a very great capacity to love unconditionally. She was brilliant and highly accomplished but never called attention to her own considerable achievements. For many years she was the head administrator of HERP, a think tank devoted to economic research at Harvard University. Music, the piano, and helping young people were her passions. In her late seventies, she became the volunteer musical director at the local high school's yearly play.

The high school students she worked with in those years became extremely devoted to her. She gave to each of them the full measure of her devotion, her considerable musical knowledge, and her unconditional love. Her love and devotion helped many of those kids flower and find their way in life. Their growth, in turn, expanded my mother's joy and delight in life. My mother is gone now, but her legacy lives on in all the lives she touched and changed and in all the good she did while she was here.

Learning to love unconditionally is a long-term process. We don't emotionally ripen over night. To love unconditionally, we must first be whole in our selves. Otherwise, we will lack the ability to set aside our personal involvement and focus on serving others. Getting to wholeness takes time. It is a process that can't be rushed or forced. Everyone has a different pace in their emotional development. Because of the differences in our pacing, it is difficult to predict when the second ego death will occur.

The Surrendered Ego

When the healthy ego finally dies and becomes the surrendered ego, one particular change provides great relief to the person who has attained the third ego level. The surrendered ego does not struggle against itself, as the ego struggled against itself in both of its earlier incarnations. The surrendered ego is defined by peace and clarity, not by conflict and confusion. The revelation of our true identity and higher purpose occurs in the surrendered ego state. It takes two ego deaths and three ego states before we know who we really are.

Raising Kundalini Has Real Risks

When we clear our body of the toxic energy that has polluted it, the raising of the Kundalini energy from its source at the base of the spine is sure and true. It will travel easily and naturally into the central gateway of the spinal canal. As the Kundalini energy rises, it increases the vibratory rate of all the chakras from the first chakra at the base of the spine to the seventh chakra above the top of the head. As each of the chakras begins to turn on a higher spiral of power, we become more magnetic, more positive, and more creative. Our immune system also becomes stronger. With more spiritual energy running through our system we have more to give to life. People who know who they really are possess a deep sense of peace and a sure sense of their destiny.

If we have not cleared the hidden toxicity from our system, however, it is highly probable that a large amount of congested energies still remains in our pelvic and hip areas. In addition, there may well be significant areas of toxic congestion in other parts of our body. For example, it is very common to have toxic energy warehoused in the stomach, heart, back, lungs, liver, kidneys, throat, and jaws. These areas of congestion break the will, prevent the Kundalini from rising, and keep the first and sixth chakras from uniting.

𝒇 If we try to raise the Kundalini before we clear our toxicity, the most common result is that we will have little, or nothing, to show for our efforts. However, if we do succeed in raising the Kundalini energy under these adverse conditions, it may very well go into one of the two minor channels that exist to the right and left of the central gateway in the spinal column.

The right channel is called Ida, the left channel Pingala. When the Kundalini rises in either channel, it may result in extreme fluctuations of bodily temperature. If the Kundalini goes up the left side of the spine and enters the Pingala channel, it will result in our feeling ice cold all the time. If the Kundalini goes up the right side of the spine and enters the Ida channel, it will result in our feeling constantly on fire. Either extreme of temperature can persist for years with no lessening of intensity. At best, either condition is highly destabilizing. At worst, either condition can result in death.

Since real dangers do exist if we attempt to raise the Kundalini energy before we are ready, it is best not to try to do so until we have cleared our toxicity. Blocked toxic energy often diverts the Kundalini energy away from the central canal, where it rises safely, and into the subsidiary channels along either side of the spine, where it can be harmful. Raising the Kundalini and unifying the will belong to the Elevation Zone and should not be attempted until the requirements of the first two growth zones have been fulfilled.

Meditation

Meditation is the primary vehicle for raising the Kundalini energy. Meditation also quiets the conscious mind, helps integrate the physical and supra-physical poles of our system, and allows the intuition, the voice of the soul, to be heard. The following two meditations will help you integrate your system, raise your Kundalini energy, and listen to the quiet voice of your soul. The first meditation can be practiced in all three zones of the path of conscious evolution. In fact, it should be done daily. The first meditation will center and balance you. It only requires a few minutes to do. The second meditation is best left for the time when you reach the Integration and Elevation Zones. It will help you integrate and unify your will.

Meditation One: Spiritual Alignment

1. Sit comfortably with your feet on the floor or in a meditative position.

2. Close your eyes. Inhale and exhale three times, breathing in deeply through your abdomen and then exhaling slowly.

3. As you conclude your third breath, imagine a ball of bright white light, like a small sun, sitting directly above the top of your head. Focus on the ball of light for a moment. As you focus on the ball of light, imagine it growing brighter and more powerful.

4. Visualize a beam from that ball of light flowing down into the top of your head and filling your entire head with a bright white light.

5. As the bright white light fills your head, allow it to flow easily through your entire body. Take as much time as you need to feel the light flowing through your body.

6. Now imagine there is a dial in your mind that can measure the intensity of the light that is flowing through your body. The highest number on this dial is seven. You are now at one. Imagine that as you turn up the number on the dial, the intensity and brightness of the light in your body increases in like manner. Now turn up the dial in your mind from one to two, then up to three, up to four, up to five, up to six, and finally up to seven, the highest level of brightness. As you reach seven, take a moment and allow the energy in your body to circulate at this highest level of brightness.

7. Now focus your attention on the center of your forehead. Allow the energy to build at this point.

8. As the energy in your forehead increases, say the following alignment aloud or in your own mind.

"My spirit, soul, mind, physical body, and emotional body are in perfect alignment with one another. I am all one, perfectly balanced, and attuned to the voice of my soul. I am guided and protected in all that I do by Divine Grace. The choices I make and the experiences I have accelerate my evolution. My soul leads me to triumph and success. All the good that I am capable of receiving appears in its perfect time."

9. Take a deep breath. Relax your focus and open your eyes.

Meditation Two: Unifying the Will

This second meditation can help you activate your will. Again, the time to practice this meditation is after you complete the tasks of the first two zones of the path of conscious evolution.

1. Begin by sitting in a semi-lotus meditative posture or in a straight-backed chair with your feet firmly on the floor.

2. Close your eyes. Take three slow deep breaths. With each exhale allow your body to relax more deeply.

3. As you complete your third breath, imagine that there is a four-sided white pyramid just above the top of your head.

4. Now imagine that the pyramid expands around you so that you are sitting inside it. The base of the pyramid sits squarely on the floor. As you sit inside the pyramid, imagine a beam of white light flowing down from its apex. This beam of light enters your head, filling your head and neck with white light. The beam of white light then flows gently down into your chest and stomach, filling these regions of your body with white light. The white light now continues to flow easily

through the rest of your body, flowing down into your hips, your legs, and your feet, filling these areas completely with light. As your trunk and legs fill with white light, the light begins to flow across your shoulders, down your arms, and into your hands. Take a moment and feel how light your entire body now feels. Let the light continue to build and circulate throughout every cell of your body. As the white light builds in your body, it gets brighter and brighter. Every cell is filled with light.

5. Now see the light expanding beyond your physical body for three feet in all directions so that you are sitting in a brilliant sphere of white light. Focus on the sphere for a moment, and imagine the light around you growing even brighter and more vibrant.

6. Now focus on your crown chakra, located just above the top of your head. The crown chakra is shaped like a wheel, lying in a horizontal position just above the top of your head. Imagine that a beam of white light flows down from the top of the pyramid and enters your crown chakra, filling it with energy and expanding it. As the crown chakra fills with light and expands, it begins to spin much more rapidly.

7. Now imagine that the beam of white light continues to move down through the remaining six charkas, filling and expanding each one in succession with white light. The third eye chakra now fills with light, expands, and begins to spin much more rapidly. The throat chakra fills with light, expands, and begins to spin much more rapidly. The heart chakra fills with light, expands, and begins to spin much more rapidly. The solar plexus chakra fills with light, expands, and begins to spin much more rapidly. The second chakra fills with light, expands, and begins to spin much more rapidly. Finally, the root chakra fills with light, expands, and begins to spin much more rapidly. These chakras resemble spinning wheels of light and are aligned vertically to their corresponding locations in the physical body.

8. All seven chakras are now filled with light. Take a deep breath, and as you exhale, allow them to synchronize with each other. The chakras are now in perfect balance. Take a moment and feel the harmony and lightness growing within you.

9. Imagine that the white light now enters your body at the base of your spine. As the white light enters your body it is transformed, becoming the color of a bright red/gold luminous flame, the color of the Kundalini energy. Concentrate for a moment on the red/gold flame, and see the Kundalini fire building in strength, heat, and intensity at the base of your spine.

10. Now take a deep breath, and as you exhale, release the Kundalini energy upward into the central gateway of the spinal column, allowing it to flow into each chakra in succession, from the root chakra at the bottom of the central gateway to the crown chakra at the top of the gateway. As the Kundalini energy surges through the spinal column, it may change colors as it enters each chakra. This is normal, and if this does occur, simply note the shift in colors as the Kundalini proceeds from chakra to chakra.

11. Now focus your attention on the third eye center at the middle of your forehead, and let the energy build in this center for a moment. As the energy builds here, imagine a tunnel of white light starting at the center of your forehead and continuing beyond your physical body for as far as your eye can see. Take a deep breath, and as you exhale, begin to walk down this tunnel of light. As you begin to walk down the tunnel, let go of your body and your orientation in time and space. Focus on the brightness of the white light all around you and the peace it brings you. Walk as far down the tunnel as you can comfortably go. Be an explorer. See where the light takes you. Take your time. You are safe and protected. Be open to what you experience. If there is something you would like to ask of your inner self,

ask it now. Observe what thoughts and impressions come back to you as you ask your question. They will contain your answer.

12. Now take another deep breath and, as you exhale, return to your physical body. Take another deep breath and ground yourself in your body as you exhale. Open your eyes and slowly reacquaint yourself with your surroundings. This completes the meditation.

Creating Peace and Balance

There are literally thousands of meditations and breathing techniques that can help you center yourself and become more peaceful. One breathing technique that I particularly like comes from the ancient Taoist tradition of China and can be done in almost any situation.

To begin the exercise, place four fingers of either hand on your lower stomach, with your index finger on your navel. Make a mental note of the point where your little finger touches your lower abdomen. The location of your little finger is actually in close proximity to an acupuncture point called Guanyuan (RN4), which means Gate of Origin. Breathing in and out slowly and rhythmically from this point builds positive energy, relieves stress, clears the mind, and creates inner peace.

To do this exercise, inhale naturally and easily, filling your diaphragm with air at the Guanyuan point, or where your little finger is located. When you do this technique correctly, your lower abdomen will expand slightly with each inhale and compress slightly with each exhale. The breath should not be forced, but easy and natural. While you are breathing in this manner, keep your mind focused on the Guanyuan point (four fingers beneath your navel) as best you can. You will find that this is not as easy as it sounds. Your mind will wander. When you become aware that your mind is wandering, re-focus it on the Guanyuan point.

As you breathe in and out, count your exhales, not your inhales. When you have reached the tenth exhale, start a new series of counting ten breaths. Keep breathing abdominally in this manner, counting your exhales from one to ten, and focusing your mind on the Guanyuan acupuncture point for fifteen to twenty minutes. That's all there is to the exercise. You can keep your eyes open or closed while doing this exercise. Don't worry about finding the absolute location of the Guanyuan point. As long as you are breathing in and out of the area on, or surrounding, this point, you will be doing this exercise correctly.

When I practiced this exercise on a regular basis, I found that for the first nine minutes of the exercise I was restless and would have to force myself to stay with it. Those first nine minutes took effort. When I hit the nine-minute mark, it seemed that a switch automatically clicked in my nervous system. From that point on I wasn't doing the technique, it was doing me. There was no more restlessness and no more struggles, just an overriding experience of peace and contentment. After those first nine minutes passed, I never wanted to stop doing the exercise. I felt like I could do it forever. I derived a great deal of peace and clarity from this exercise.

If you do this exercise in the morning, you will find that it will energize you for the whole day, giving you clarity, peace, and energy. If you do it before you go to bed, you will find that it helps you sleep deeply.

Techniques and the Path

In general, I think that when it comes to techniques, the fewer one uses, the better. Techniques can help us balance our energies, reduce stress, maintain a calm center, and keep a clear head. However, techniques should never be used as a substitute for experiencing life or as an excuse for not facing one's shadow. Ultimately, we learn more from our life experiences than from whatever techniques we might employ to manage our life.

The Buddha once said, "You can't travel on the path until you become the path itself." The person who has awakened from his slumber and become the person he was meant to be has become that path. He is whole and guided by his soul. The person who builds his life on techniques is still searching for his way. He has not digested and transformed his life experiences nor learned the lessons from those experiences that he must. His ego is still in command. He has neither awakened his Kundalini nor unified his will.

The Distant Future

Sometime in the far distant future, humanity will evolve to the place where everyone has a unified will as well as a fused soul and ego, and has become a channel for unconditional love, in much the same way that everyone now has a conscious mind and the potential for rational thought. While that higher reality is merely embryonic in the human race at present, the very real possibility exists that each of us who so chooses can manifest that higher reality in our lifetime.

Some people are very close to being Self-realized, while others are farther away from knowing who they are. Whether we are close to that state or far from it, one thing is certain. It won't happen on its own. We have to choose to make it happen. If we don't choose to discover our true identity, then whatever distance we may be from that realization does not matter. Near or far is the same distance of failure.

If we do choose to pursue our growth and seek our true identity, then close and far do matter. When we are close, the end result is surer, but it is not necessarily easier to achieve. There are always many challenges on the road to realization. The Buddha, for example, was born very close to full Self-realization. It was sleeping just below the surface of his conscious mind, but in order to get to that realization, he had to renounce all he had, wander in the forest for years, and try many false paths before he discovered his true way.

Form and Essence

The great mystical poet Rumi once wrote that,

> *He who knows not, and knows not that he knows not, is a fool—shun him.*
> *He who knows not, and knows that he knows not, is a child—teach him.*
> *He who knows and knows not that he knows is asleep—wake him!*

But he who knows, and knows that he knows, is a wise man—follow him.

To help illuminate the difference between knowing and not knowing, let us examine the distinction between form and essence. In spiritual practice, a form is what we use to reach our essence. For instance, we might do Hatha Yoga and meditate on a mantra, or do Tai Chi and meditate on our breath. We might pursue an intellectual path of discrimination, an emotional path of devotion, an active path of service, or a meditative path of contemplation. The point is that there are many paths and many ways to the center of our being, all of them valid and each of them helpful.

The problem occurs when we confuse form with essence and then substitute form for realization. Just because we are doing Yoga, meditating, or chanting does not mean that we have discovered who we really are or found our true-life purpose. Doing Yoga does not equal realization. Our involvement in a spiritual form does not mean that our practice of that form has necessarily evolved us or taken us to the center of our being, as many people assume it has because they feel relatively more peaceful. Doing Yoga is just doing Yoga. It does not equal automatic Self-realization. Spiritual glamour comes about when we confuse our involvement in a form with Self-realization. Spiritual glamour strengthens the negative ego rather than subduing it.

Many people make the assumption that because they have started the journey and feel more peaceful they have arrived at the journey's end. These are the people that Rumi called fools when he spoke of those who know not, and know not that they know not. Form does not equal essence. An acquaintance of mine once put this same idea in a slightly different context. He said that when a person thinks he has arrived, he has, because he is not going any farther.

The Four Requirements of Identity

How, then, will we know when we have reached our center and discovered our true identity? That's a fair and important question and not an easy one to answer. True identity is impossible to define, largely because it is not a material thing, like a rock, a box, a house, or a body. True identity connects us to the world beyond this world. True identity is housed in the soul and spirit, not based in the body, brain, or ego. Our true identity merges with our conscious mind when our spiritual nervous system is clear and balanced, our Kundalini has been released, and we know how to love unconditionally.

There are four requirements that we must meet before our identity will be revealed to us.

- ✧ *We must clear our toxicity.*

- ✧ *Fuse our soul and ego.*

- ✧ *Unify our will.*

- ✧ *Become a channel for unconditional love.*

While these are all big tasks, they are not impossible ones. Sri Aurobindo, the great twentieth century Indian spiritual master, was fond of saying that a complete transformation takes, "everything we have and everything we are, but nothing more."

In my own case that was certainly true. Over a ten-year period, I lost many people I loved dearly and many of my possessions. How I chose to deal with the extremely difficult challenges of those years changed and evolved me more than anything else possibly could have. The life trials I endured brought me closer to my essence than any spiritual form ever could have. I was thrown into a great purifying fire that burned me to my core and destroyed my former life.

The Moment of Truth

Many times, it is not until much later that we see the real value in what life has forced us to face. Beauty is often born from pain, and transcendence frequently results from an unexpected descent into darkness. If the transformational journey teaches us anything, it is that we cannot ascend until we complete our descent, that we cannot elevate our life until we first clear it of its toxic content. The road to fulfillment begins when we face the manner in which we are unfulfilled. The road to true identity starts when we confront our notions of whom we think we are but in reality, are not.

If we choose to make the effort to transform our lives, we will also be participating in the larger transformation of the planet, whether we know it or not. Whenever someone opens to the radiance in his soul, the world benefits from the spiritual light that opening brings to the planet. When we open ourselves to the light from above we create new opportunities in our own life, and we become a blessing to the world.

Whenever someone becomes a channel for unconditional love, the world becomes a brighter and safer place. Whenever someone unifies his will, the world moves closer to the truth. Whenever someone realizes his true identity, it makes it easier for everyone else to do so.

We are the pioneers. Our footprints on the future will be large. What we do now counts more than ever. The clock is ticking, the hour late. This is not a time for apathy. If we choose the path of personal evolution, we will make it easier for everyone in the future to follow in our footsteps. There is no task greater than this or any work that is as necessary.

We stand at a pivotal moment of truth. Will we defeat the epidemics of our time? Can we step back from the fast moving cycles of hatred, polarization, and conflict that threaten to overwhelm the world? Can the light inside us defeat the darkness already afoot in the world? Will enough of us choose the path of personal evolution and create the critical mass in consciousness necessary to shift the world into a better future?

The Power of Prayer

If ever there was a time for prayer, that time is now. Prayer, like meditation, is primarily a tool of the Elevation Zone, although it can be practiced in any zone of the journey. In meditation we quiet the mind, establish contact with the soul, and attune ourselves to the light of the spirit. In prayer, we ask the Divine energy to accomplish specific tasks.

The prayers of someone who has cleared his toxicity, fused his soul and ego, unified his will, and become a channel of unconditional love are more powerful than the prayers of someone who has not yet transformed his consciousness. The more light and spiritual power, sincerity, clarity, and love we bring to prayer, the greater is the possibility that our prayers will be answered.

We should pray for the world to find its center, as we work to find our own. We should pray for world peace and to be at peace with ourselves. We should pray to be an instrument of unconditional love and compassion. We should pray for those who are less fortunate than we are and in need of assistance. We should pray quietly and without overt display, and we should pray often.

The Scientific Effect of Prayer

Several studies have shown that those who pray regularly live longer than those who do not. Prayer and meditation lower blood pressure and contribute to a healthier immune system. Prayer enhances our ability to cope with difficult and demanding situations. It makes us feel less alone in the world, and less helpless.

If we transform our lives, we will find our personal strength, and we will find an even greater strength in union with the Divine. We will be able to stand on our own, and in our truth, no matter the challenge, no matter the cost. When we arrive where we must and know who we really are, nothing will stop us from moving forward to build a better life and a better world.

Life's Great Opportunity

The chance to grow is the great opportunity life grants each of us. The chance to grow is also the only real equality we will find in life. We are all in different circumstances with different talents, strengths, and weaknesses, and are all at different levels of evolution. Regardless of the situation we are in, growth from that place is always possible. The tragedy of life is that so few people seize their opportunities to transform themselves.

My grandfather was a teacher and a scholar. Back in the nineteen fifties and sixties, he would often stop his car in the neighborhood when he saw children playing in the street. He would tell those children to be careful, stay out of trouble, dream big, and do good things with their lives, for they were the hope of the world.

Those children are all grown up now. They are you and I. They are our children, and our children's children. We are all the hope of the world, and it is time for us to accept our high calling. Let us clear our toxicity, open our minds to the light, discover who we are, and become channels of unconditional love. If we do that, everything we need will arrive in its appointed time.

The Divine in each of us is the Way, the Truth, and the Light. While we are all different on the personality level, we all share in the great gifts of the spirit. The main difference between us is that only a few have actualized those gifts, while the rest have not. The secret to true equality between people is Self-realization. The secret to a real and lasting peace in the world is Self-realization. The secret to abundance for all is Self-realization.

When we open the door to the Divine, we enter the greatest mystery of life. In that moment, the Divine power pours into the chalice of the human soul, and the eternal and the temporal become one. It is the moment of most power, a time of great quickening in which our potential is actualized and our identity realized. When that moment arrives we will never be the same as we once were. The old life will be over, the old karma swept away. We'll be deeper, happier, infinitely more peaceful, and fulfilled.

May life bring you to your true self. May your true self lead you to your true purpose. May your true purpose lead you to fulfillment. May the fulfillment of your purpose help many others find their way. For if enough of us find our way, the world will find its way.

℘℘℘

Lord, make me an instrument of Your peace,
Where there is hatred, let me sow love;
Where there is injury, pardon;
Where there is doubt, faith;
Where there is darkness, light;
And where there is sadness, joy;
O, Divine Master,
Grant that I may not so much seek
To be consoled, as to console;
To be understood as to understand;
To be loved as to love;
For it is in giving that we receive;
It is in pardoning that we are pardoned;
And it is in dying that we are born to eternal life.

St Frances of Assisi, *Serenity Prayer*

℘℘℘

More books and cds by Alan Mesher...
Open yourself to a greater light and harness the higher power.

Books
Journey of Love: A formula for Mastery and Miracles
The T Zone: The Path to Inner Power
The T Zone is a special book about inner growth and spiritual transformation for those who want to heal their lives and reach for the highest potential within themselves.

Cds
Harmony and Balance

Vitality

Listen to the deeply enchanting music of talented Hollywood composer Lindsay Gillis. Feel the incredible spiritual power of Alan Mesher.

ginger tea 3 times a day

chai

Dr. Oz. exercise (monday)
increase (Supplement) 8

WWW.DR.OZ.COM

cambridge eye doctors

1. hyloris acid

2. 2 tbsp honey
2. yogurt

Give the gift of
Just Who Do You Think You Are?
and other books and cds by Alan Mesher to friends, family members, and colleagues

Check your local bookstore or order here:

☐ **Yes**, send _____ copies of *Just Who Do You Think You Are?* .... 19.95 ea
California residents add sales tax per copy 1.65

☐ **Yes**, send _____ copies of *The T Zone: The Path to Inner Power* ..... 14.95 ea
California residents add sales tax per copy 1.23

☐ **Yes**, send _____ copies of healing cd *Harmony and Balance* .... 29.95 ea
California residents add sales tax per copy 2.47

☐ **Yes**, send _____ copies of cd *Vitality* .... 29.95 ea
California residents add sales tax per copy 2.47

Shipping & handling   one book or cd 3.95
each additional book or cd 1.95

California residents must include 8.25% sales tax as calculated above.
Canadian orders must include payment in US funds, with 7% GST added.
Payment must accompany orders. Please allow 3 weeks for delivery.

Total _____

Make your checks payable and return to:
Sirius Creations
P.O. Box 1290
Pacific Palisades, CA 90272

You may also place your orders on the internet at www.siriuscreations.com
or by credit card:

Name _____ Organization _____
Address _____
City/State/Zip _____
Phone _____ E-Mail _____
Credit Card # _____ Exp. Date _____
Signature _____

☐ **Yes** I am interested in having Alan Mesher speak or give a seminar to
my company, association, school, church or organization. Please
send me information.